I0044494

GOLD IN THE GOLDEN YEARS

How to Create a Successful Business
with the S.O.A.R. Launch and Grow Plan
to Fulfill Your Purpose and Passion
to Make Your Own Gold!

Special Features for Women Over Fifty

GOLD IN THE GOLDEN YEARS

How to Create a Successful Business
with the S.O.A.R. Launch and Grow Plan
to Fulfill Your Purpose and Passion
to Make Your Own Gold!

Special Features for Women Over Fifty

Nan McKay

Published by Best Seller Publishing®, St. Augustine, FL
Best Seller Publishing® is a registered trademark.
Printed in the United States of America.
ISBN: 978-1-956649-86-4

For more information, please write:
Best Seller Publishing®
53 Marine Street
St. Augustine, FL 32084
or call 1 (626) 765-9750

Visit us online at:
www.BestSellerPublishing.org

TABLE OF CONTENTS

FOREWORD

YOUR PASSION IS NOT AN ACCIDENT

BY KIM WALSH PHILLIPS

It was more than a decade ago, but I remember it as clearly as yesterday. I was leaning against the doorway of a designer-clad kitchen, feeling exhausted from my first trimester of pregnancy but excited for what lay ahead.

My feet were swollen. My waistband felt tight. Yet I was happier than I ever remembered being.

I had just shared my happy news of impending motherhood with a dear friend, who also happened to be the first physician general of Pennsylvania, Dr. Wanda Filer. An amazing woman. She gave me a sage piece of advice that I still follow when it comes to motherhood and career:

"Never tell your kids you *have to go to work*. Share instead, *I get to go* and make an impact today." Brilliant.

To this day, each night at my house we go around the family dinner table asking, "Who did you impact today?" After everyone else shares, I reveal who else my family impacted that day through their support of my work.

From the sheer numbers and reach of celebrities I've been able to work with—like Kevin O'Leary from *Shark Tank* and his Shark Tank investments to NFL athletes like Chris Gronkowski, to the Nat King Cole Foundation, to folks you never heard of before, like one of my coaches who helps parents to calm the tantrums, to another who saves teens from the perils of the dark web, and another who helps attorneys grow their practice, to yet another who teaches life skills to inner city girls—I serve thousands of people each year, and because my family members support my purpose, I can in turn support those I coach, and in turn they can support others.

It is the most incredible way to make a living, and to *make a life*. It allows me to tap into things that bring me joy each and every day.

Even though this work has afforded me a lifestyle that is quite different from that of how I grew up—living in abundance instead of scarcity, being able to provide my kids the things I only dreamed of, and supporting charities that are important to me—that is not what brings me the most joy. (Side note: The person who said that money doesn't bring you happiness must not have known how to make an impact with that cash.)

My favorite moments are when I see others uncover their impact-driven success. My joy soars when they realize that what they already love to do is actually what they are being called to do.

Because I know this to be true, our passions are not an accident: they are our God-given superpowers, and when we lean into them, not only do we find our purpose, but we also find our joy.

And we unlock the treasure that's been inside us all along.

There is good news waiting for you in the pages of this book. Wouldn't it be incredible to do this, no matter your age, past, or lack of experience? What if you could lean into who you are and why you were created, so that you could serve others in a meaningful way that is both profitable and pleasurable?

Sounds good, right?

Well, this book gives you the exact path to show you how. Nan McKay has launched six businesses, one of which staffs over 2000 people. She is the ultimate resource for starting and growing a business you love.

As Tony Robbins says, "If you want to be successful, find someone who has achieved the results you want and copy what they do, and you'll achieve the same results."

You've just found your blueprint.

Use this book as your starting point to discover what's possible and what's been waiting inside of you all along. Then get ready to multiply your impact and income.

Because you, my friend, were made to thrive.

Kim Walsh Phillips, Founder and CEO
Powerful Professionals

* * *

Kim Walsh Phillips

Kim Walsh Phillips is the founder of Powerful Professionals, a business coaching and education company. She went from thirty-two clients to over eleven thousand in less than a year and was recently named 475th in the *Inc.* 5000 and is an MBA-free self-made millionaire.

Named "a must to read by those in business" by *Forbes* magazine, she is the bestselling author of multiple books including *The Ultimate Guide to Instagram for Business* and *The No B.S. Guide to Direct Response Social Media Marketing.*

She's the behind-the-scenes secret weapon of some of the biggest names in business, including Kevin O'Leary from *Shark Tank*, Dan Kennedy, *Profit First* author Mike Michalowicz, Harley-Davidson, Hilton Hotels, and High Point University, and has spoken onstage beside some of the world's leading thought leaders including Tony Robbins, Grant Cardone, Barbara Corcoran, and Gary Vaynerchuk.

She resides just outside of Atlanta, Georgia, with her very tall husband and glitter-obsessed girls, and is fueled by faith, love, laughter, and lots and lots (and lots) of coffee.

Find out more about Kim and her programs at
powerfulprofessionals.com

FOREWORD

OLDER WOMEN ROCK!

BY MARLENE WAGMAN-GELLER

Women who came of age or were born in the midcentury U.S. have more to worry about than loss of pigment, varicose veins, and crepey cleavage. These women are the nonfictional Mrs. Cunninghams, the mother in *Happy Days* who spent her days putting others' needs above her own. However, unlike their television counterparts, many modern-day matrons are facing unhappy days because of their precarious financial situations. One source of their lack of financial savvy is that they grew up in an era that taught them not to worry their pretty little heads about economic matters; after all, that was the domain of fathers and husbands. Subsequently, girls understood how to spend, but they were in the dark on how to earn, how to save.

Back in the day, married women could not open a bank account or obtain a credit card without their spouse's approval. The Holy Grail of matrimony was looking after family, and therefore, society frowned upon the women who seemingly put loved ones on the back burner. Another reason the term "working woman" raised eyebrows was the assumption that she was only doing so because hubby had failed in his role as provider. Thus, a woman's earning a paycheck equaled emasculation. Given their social straightjackets, women became wizards in the kitchens, perfected the art of the bouffant. As the roadmap only showed life as a housewife, few women aspired to post-secondary education. After all, how much education does it take to read a recipe?

Fast-forward to today, and it becomes all too apparent that there was something wrong with the pretty picture of the past. For Mrs. Cunningham, her husband remained her economic trampoline, but thousands of women are not so fortunate. The danger of not having economic autonomy shows up when life does not go as planned. What happens to the first wife when her husband leaves her for the trophy wife? What happens to the widows whose easy street hits a road block when their husbands pass away? What happens to the Mrs. when the Mr. loses their nest egg in a mid-life crisis? The answer to these questions may be found by reading Nan McKay's entrepreneurial bible, *Gold in the Golden Years.*

My life intersected with Nan's when she interviewed me for her podcast, "TrailBlazers Impact," to discuss two of my books that deal with the theme of female empowerment. The first was *Women Who Launch: Women Who Shattered Glass Ceilings.* The premise of the book is to showcase women who launched iconic enterprises such as Estée Lauder, who founded a cosmetics empire; Ruth Handler who created Barbie; or Sara Blakely, whose Spanx empire made her *Forbes*-worthy. My second book, *Great Second Acts: In Praise of Older Women,* does its best to destroy the mindset of "the old gray mare, she ain't what she used to be." Some of the awe-inspiring women of a certain age profiled include Golda Meir, who became Israel's first prime minister at age seventy; Shirley Temple Black, who became the American ambassador to Czechoslovakia at age sixty-one; and Madeleine Albright, who became the Secretary of State at age sixty.

One of the questions I posed to Nan for the purpose of writing this foreword was how she had bypassed the financial pitfall that many women in her age demographic had fallen into. Nan discusses this in her book, starting with:

For me, that significant emotional event occurred at age eleven. We went from an above-average lifestyle to being the pariahs in a small town of 3,000 people. My high-living father was killed in a car accident, along with three other people. He had newly purchased a Jaguar, a fast sports car, and was giving a ride to the son of a prominent family. We discovered he was a gambler afterward, when many people called us, asking for their money. Because we were the relatives left, we paid for his last act. My brother was six and my sister was three months old.

The rest of the story is in her book.

She explains her second reason:

I married a guy (second marriage but we've been married 53 years) who wasn't a take-charge, risk-taker, task-oriented person like I am, but instead was very supportive. When I started traveling 40 weeks a year (which I did for 30 years), he was the glue that held the family together to raise two kids who I am very close to today. I missed a lot of birthdays and school conferences, but the family held together and both have a strong work ethic today—and are good kids! Marriage has been a team effort every step of the way.

Nan McKay has worn any number of professional hats: entrepreneur, government employee, podcaster, and author, the last of which she undertook to help women on the road to financial and personal fulfillment wellness. I highly recommend *Gold in the Golden Years* for anyone who needs a how-to book on the process of getting one's financial and personal life back on track. Great Second Acts wait for those with the courage to change an old paradigm, one that no longer is doing the proverbial trick.

I want to conclude this foreword with the tagline from *Great Second Acts:* Older women do not need rocking chairs; they rock!

* * *

Marlene Wagman-Geller

Marlene Wagman-Geller is a best-selling author on *Empowered Women*. She is the author of several books, including *Once Again to Zelda: The Stories Behind Literature's Most Intriguing Dedications* (Perigree/Penguin 2008), *Eureka!: The Surprising Stories Behind the Ideas That Shaped the World* (Perigree/Penguin 2010), *And the Rest Is History: The Famous (and Infamous) First Meetings of the World's Most Passionate Lovers* (Perigree/Penguin 2011), *Behind Every Great Man: The Forgotten Women Behind the world's Famous and Infamous* (Source Books 2015), *Still I Rise: The Persistence of Phenomenal Women* (Mango Press 2017), *Women Who Launch: Women Who Shattered Glass Ceilings* (Mango Press 2018), *Great Second Acts: In Praise of Older Women* (Mango Press 2018), *Women of Means: Fascinating Biographies of Royals, Heiresses, Eccentrics and Other Poor Little Rich Girls* (Mango Press 2019), and *Fabulous Female Firsts: Because of Them We Can* (Mango Press 2020). *The New York Times*, *Chicago Tribune*, and *Washington Post* have reviewed her books.

Wagman-Geller received her BA from York University and her teaching credentials from the University of Toronto and San Diego State University. She currently teaches high school English in National City, California, and lives with her family—along with cat, Moe, and dog, Harley—in San Diego.

PROLOGUE

Are you ready for a change? Are you excited to take on a new challenge? Is this point in life the time to dust yourself off and start all over again? This book is your key to pivoting toward freedom, providing options for flexibility, and allowing you the opportunity to take charge of your own life. The book, broken down into four sections with easy steps, will help you stay focused, organized, and ensure your right path.

But why listen to me? Who am I? After working seventeen years for government agencies, I started Nan McKay and Associates, Inc., in 1980 with $10,000 from cashing out my retirement account. Nan McKay and Associates, one of the six businesses I founded over the years, is now a multimillion-dollar company with 2,000 staff. Some of the businesses were wildly successful. One was a dismal failure. Empowering women to succeed through adversity has been my passion for many years. Having taught executive management classes to thousands of people across the country and having been through the highs and lows of starting my own businesses, my lessons learned will help you avoid the mistakes I made. Yes, you too can succeed in business at any age by following my proven formula as you discover who you are, what you want to do, and how you want to do it.

Although I am President of Nan McKay and Associates, I started another business, Nan McKay Connects (NMC). NMC is a business consulting and media company with its mission being to empower the new beautiful generation of women over 50 to dare to take the next steps to reach the lifestyle of their dreams and bring out their brilliance.

Gold in the Golden Years includes two special features. You will meet a variety of knowledgeable and experienced women who share their experiences and insights with you as excerpts from their personal interviews from the TrailBlazers Impact podcasts and videos. These women are all successful entrepreneurs. They have started their own businesses, in some cases without any help. You will find interesting information within their true stories of experience and expertise. Their complete interviews are available at https://nanmckayconnects.com.

In addition, contributing guest authors share their knowledge and expertise on critical topics. Should you want additional information about any of them, their website information is available on their individual guest page on https://nanmckayconnects.com.

The best recipe for your success is to explore who you are and what you want by developing an action plan, which leads you on your personal journey of discovery. Stop in every chapter, grab something to drink, place yourself in a quiet space where you can think, and complete the action plan step for that chapter. These steps guide you from an idea to a finished product by leading you to draw conclusions, helping you develop an action plan for implementation.

Our special gift to you is a bonus, which is full of wonderful surprises! You can link to the bonus here:
https://nanmckayconnects.com/goldpowerbonus.

Whether you pivot from a career, like I did, or are retired and looking for fulfillment in your life, starting a business may be the answer for you to move forward into a second act—and make money while you do it! If you have ever thought of starting a business, your action plan will help you lay out an empowerment plan, taking you from wherever you are right now to driving your passion, purpose, and profit by launching and growing your own woman-owned lifestyle business after fifty.

Come with me on the journey and *refire*!

GOLD IN THE GOLDEN YEARS

GOLD POWER BONUS!

Get over $2661 worth of bonuses including...

FAST ACTION BONUS

- **Leadership Skills Cheat Sheet**
- **Facebook Checklist for Business**
- **How to Build a Targeted Email List**
- **How to Create a Positive Work Environment**
- **10 Tips to Pivot to Entrepreneurship**
- **Facebook Marketing Made Easy**
- **25 Online Business Ideas**
- **Master Class 5X Your Followers by Kim Walsh Phillips: https://powerfulprofessionals.com/5xformula**
- **Course: Is Entrepreneurship Right for You? (Use Code: FREE)**
- **And more...**

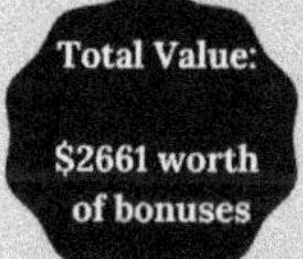

https://nanmckayconnects.com/goldpowerbonus

And make your life easy! Register for our course, Gold in the Golden Years MasterClass, and you can work through this blueprint step by step. Nan hosts a monthly group meeting with this class so you can focus on your Action Plan Workbook with her.

SECTION I

S.O.A.R.: SELECT YOUR GOALS AND CHOOSE A BUSINESS

CHAPTER 1

PIVOT TO FREEDOM, FLEXIBILITY, AND FINANCIAL INDEPENDENCE

The strong voice inside says, "I could start a business, and through hard work, achieve financial rewards large enough to sustain my lifestyle. But how? What type of business would I choose? What are the risks and the rewards?" And the dreaded thought that still lingers: "Am I too old?"

Women over fifty want to own the passion they feel bubbling up inside. Women want financial independence and the freedom and flexibility to forge their path through their life's journey. *Gold in the Golden Years* will take you on a personal journey to discover whether entrepreneurship holds the key to the gold for you. Best of all, you will have the secret map—the blueprint—to the gold.

The purpose of the S.O.A.R. Launch and Growth Plan is to guide you through your discovery journey, providing action steps and research resources. A feature of this book includes insights from trailblazers who have transitioned from a financially secure full-time job to entrepreneurship, insights from trailblazers who have retired to start a business of their own, and insights from women in the corporate world speaking on creating a leadership role in your new business. Following the S.O.A.R. Launch and Growth Plan creates an experience and a plan to mitigate the risk by guiding you to lay out a clear path to follow. No single path provides exact steps everyone should follow, and success has no deadline. Assurance of fulfillment is not guaranteed, but assurance that you can control your actions is achievable.

The four steps in the S.O.A.R. Launch and Growth Plan for successful entrepreneurship are:

- **Select** your goals, define your interests, and choose a business
- **Organize** your launch and growth to be successful and filled with joy
- **Acquire** customers with similar missions and visions
- **Realize** your destiny as you multiply your impact and income

This book will guide you from your initial idea and any indecision you may have to deciding if owning a business is for you. If your time to decide is now, you will go on to the next steps of choosing and launching a business that drives your passion, purpose, and profit. If you already have a business and need more growth and traction, the blueprint will work for you. The purpose of this book is to be the wind beneath your wings—not to tell you exactly what to do. This book is about choices and systems, and it will help you think about your plan and develop your path to see it clearly, and then you can decide whether you want to forge ahead. As you read, answer the questions in each chapter to help you formulate your Action Plan, which will help guide you along your journey to find out whether this path is right for you, and you will begin drafting your blueprint of how to meet your goals. If you want to leave a job, are getting ready to retire, are already retired, or want to start a side hustle or a full-time business to change your lifestyle, but you aren't sure where to start, this book is for you! The outcome is that you can work every day doing work you love and multiply your revenue while meeting your destiny.

First-time entrepreneurs need a clear path to how to get from the beginning to the launch. New entrepreneurs can feel overwhelmed because they are not sure what they should do next. The feeling of being overwhelmed can lead to spinning, not focusing, and can even lead to depression because the journey to entrepreneurship can sometimes seem like too much. You want to avoid those feelings, and you can! You will have the blueprint that breaks entrepreneurship knowledge into bite-size chunks and places everything in a more systemized pot of gold.

Do I want to replace my 9 to 5? Now that I can work remotely, is now the perfect time to build a business? How do I do that? How can I start my own business? Will I be okay? Most of us have pivoted numerous times already! When we use the word *pivot*, we think of a massive shift from one place to another. You may not realize it, but you may only be a few steps away from the change you want in your life. If you want to go forward into your new life, if you feel like things have to change, if you want to explore a new horizon, this book is for you. Do you want to work from home? Do you want to make a greater impact on the world? Do you want your money working for you? Do you want to sell what you know? Do you want to feel the rush of success? Do you want to find the right business for you? Do you want a guide for launching a business? Do you want a guide to growing your business?

Working hard at something we don't care about is called stress. Working hard for something we love is called passion. Are you ready to put the gold in the golden years? Are you prepared for a lifestyle change? Keep two outcomes in mind: love what you do and pursue what seduces you. This chapter will help you imagine your new life!

Turning fifty is a milestone in our lives. Somehow, we have crossed a defining line when we reach fifty. Today you drove by the senior housing development, now referred to as "senior living," which allows only people who are at least fifty or fifty-five to live in the development. With a start, we think, "OMG! That's me!" We feel we have paid our dues, worked hard our entire lives, and are finally grown up. Not old. Just grown up. We know our parents will never feel like we are grown up, but we know we have reached the threshold, and we can say that we are grown up. Turning fifty can be a powerful feeling, allowing us the freedom to come into our own.

Then it's sixty and seventy and eighty—and we feel lucky we are still alive and kicking! It's a shock to become our parents. For many of us who had children, they are at an age when they do not need us as much as they did when they were younger. We have more time available. We have more money than we did at thirty or even forty. We have more focus and even more discipline because we were usually the ones who kept the rest of the family on track and on schedule. We learned to organize to get our family members where they needed to be, or we bore the brunt of the consequences for our children and our spouse. We do not have the same demands on our time as we did earlier in life, which affords us more freedom to explore our options.

INSIGHTS INTO BEING OVER FIFTY

INTERVIEW WITH **ROBIN BREWTON**

https://www.linkedin.com/in/robinbrewton/
https://nanmckayconnects.com/2022/01/how-to-pivot-into-entrepreneurship-without-fear-robin-brewton/

Robin Brewton

Robin Brewton is in the early stages of her pivot to becoming an executive coach. She describes herself as being an interior designer for businesses. She explains her views on pivoting and how she got to that point. She started out in human resources, but that career was not a perfect fit for her. She was always more concerned about the revenue of the business, the operation side of the business, than she was about compensation and benefits. However, the human resources career was a natural segue for her to move into chief operating officer roles later in her career. Being able to put that awesome career together and use it at this point in her life makes a great pivot for her.

> *I wish I had learned earlier to stop thinking or worrying about what other people think. I think women are in their sweet spot. The ones you want to help so much that are over fifty are in this amazing spot where we have perhaps the financial luxury to do something different. We are at a time in life where we have fewer responsibilities around family. We're closer to knowing what our passions are. Now is the time to take that leap to say, "I finally want what I've evaded all of these years! It is finally time for me*

to make that leap!" I wish them all the best as they cross that bridge. Don't be afraid because the joys are on the other side. Make the risks well worth it.

* * *

Many of us have experienced ageism in the workplace, adding further to our desire to want to go out on our own. When we encountered this ageism, some of our thoughts went to "Should I start the lift—faces, boobs, underarms, eyes—you name it?" We thought, "If only I could find that perfect wrinkle-erase cream, I would be better seen and asked to take on the new plum project for an increase in pay."

I am over fifty, and I will tell you, "We are tired of being taken for granted! We are tired of being judged. We are tired of being passed over in our corporate life. Do those corporate executives think our minds have atrophied because we reached a certain age? Or, like a can of tuna, that we have exceeded our expiration date? What's wrong with *them*?"

Today I admit I still look in the magnifying mirror and think, "I must be sleeping on my face wrong to have all these lines." I admit I had facials every month until the pandemic hit. I admit I smear cream on my forehead where I see a tiny frown line and pull back on my ears and raise my brows to make the lines disappear. I admit I have an appointment to get some of that extra skin removed above my eyelids that I know appeared in one night. I realize I look at my underarms and pull my sleeves on my blouse down. Regardless, I will defy the bogus notion that aging women are not attractive. I will embrace my wrinkles as badges of courage, determination, and genes. After all, I have had quite a few years to earn them.

As you get older and have choices, you start to think, "What really matters to me?" As you have time to look around the world, you start to see many events that do not go the way you want them to go. According to McKinsey, at the beginning of 2020, the representation of women in corporate America was trending—albeit slowly—in the right direction. Between January 2015 and December 2019, the number of women in senior vice president positions increased from 23 to 28 percent, and in the C-suite from 17 to 21 percent.[1] Though the numbers were progressing slightly upward, women remain dramatically underrepresented, especially women of color.

You have knowledge and capabilities. You have paid your dues. Have you been on the corporate track for years? Are you stuck in the good life with the house you always wanted, the car you love to drive, but you are still not feeling satisfied? You have had some time to consider what you want to do for the rest of your life. Is what you are doing today, right now, fulfilling to you? Is what you are currently doing enough? Are you passionate about your job? A Microsoft study from June 2021 discovered that 41 percent of workers worldwide were considering quitting their jobs.[2] Are you feeling you want to start anew to live your passion? Do you feel another level is available for you to achieve to fulfill your purpose? Are you willing to settle for what you have? Or are you at the point where things must change?

If you are in the corporate world and you are over fifty, you may have observed a difference in how you are treated versus ten to twenty years ago when you first started with the company. Unfortunately, ageism is alive and well in the corporate world. This world judges your dress, your looks, your actions. Do you still feel a lack of full respect, responsibility, and financial reward enjoyed by your male colleagues of your same stature in the company? When you experience a judgmental attitude,

---

1. https://www.mckinsey.com/featured-insights/diversity-and-inclusion/seven-charts-that-show-covid-19s-impact-on-womens-employment#:~:text=Between%20January%202015%20and%20December,underrepresented%2C%20especially%20women%20of%20color.

2. Microsoft https://www.microsoft.com/en-us/worklab/work-trend-index/hybrid-work

do you feel devalued or like you are on a treadmill? Do you think life is eluding you? Do you feel an urgency to make a difference?

INSIGHTS ON GENDERED AGEISM

INTERVIEW WITH **BONNIE MARCUS**,

FOUNDER AND CEO OF BONNIE MARCUS LEADERSHIP AND AUTHOR OF *NOT DONE YET!*

https://nanmckayconnects.com/2021/07/how-to-overcome-gendered-ageism-bonnie-marcus/

Bonnie Marcus

Bonnie Marcus is an expert in gendered ageism. As an award-winning entrepreneur, *Forbes* contributing writer, and executive coach, Marcus assists professional women successfully navigate the workplace and their position and promote themselves to advance their careers.

> *Women, especially in the forty-five to fifty-plus age group, often find that they are not acknowledged or respected in the workplace. As they show visible signs of aging, they are often viewed as irrelevant and feel diminished, marginalized, and certainly unfulfilled in their careers. These women have a great track record. They've worked hard. Many of the women I have interviewed have held high positions, and suddenly they become invisible, and their workload is redistributed. Many of these women are pushed out before they want to retire, when they still have so much to offer. Some women may choose to leave the workplace on their own because they are not getting the acknowledgment or respect for their contributions. Many of those women start their own business. But for the most part, the women over fifty who remain in the corporate arena experience gendered ageism.*

* * *

INSIGHTS ON BEING UNDERESTIMATED AS A WOMAN

INTERVIEW WITH **KITTY CHANEY-REED**,

VICE PRESIDENT OF ENTERPRISE OPERATIONS AND SENIOR STATE EXECUTIVE FOR IBM

https://nanmckayconnects.com/2021/02/kitty-chaney-reed/

Kitty Chaney-Reed

Kitty Chaney-Reed is Vice President of Enterprise Operations at IBM and Senior State Executive for IBM and Georgia. Chaney-Reed was selected for the Most Powerful and Influential Woman award from the Georgia Diversity Council, and she was named Woman of the Year for enterprise businesses with over 2,500 employees. She is an example of working effectively with others and gives us tips on how to exceed expectations when moving up the corporate ladder.

> *I would tell you that if you've been in corporate America as a woman for any period of time, you have certainly been underestimated at some point in your career. Yes, I have been underestimated. It is not something that you do something about. It is something that you respond to, and you respond to it with excellence. For me, every time I have been underestimated, I have overperformed. That, for me, is absolutely the way to respond to those who think that you cannot compete with the strongest of the bunch, or that you do not have anything to add, or you did not earn your seat at the table. You just have to demonstrate to people through outcomes and results that you earned your spot, and you are going to keep earning it.*

* * *

In your fifties in the corporate world, you cannot always rely on your track record. Do not make assumptions that may hurt you from lack of awareness. That may be your reality, but your reality may not be the corporation's reality. You are not irrelevant or powerless. You are not too old to compete! Read Bonnie Marcus's book *Not Done Yet!*[3] She will help you regain your confidence and claim workplace power. However, if you decide not to stay in the corporate world and want to explore another avenue, read on.

Statistics indicate that executive women experience long and gradually even longer workweeks. In the United States, the percentage of women working more than fifty hours a week is higher than in any other country. Women struggle to have a work-life balance when work is a high percentage of their available time. Women often feel frazzled because they are pulled in so many directions, and the result can be that everyone else is on their to-do list, but they are not. Career women over fifty are facing a double-edged sword. On one hand, they have invested many years and untold hours to achieve their place in the corporate structure and the salary that enables their current lifestyle. But, on the other hand, the feeling of being disposable is increasing. More women fear retaliation and negative impacts on their careers if they assert the need for more work-life balance. However, the demand for work-life balance grows, and women are beginning to look for an alternative. The question becomes, "If I have to work this hard and give up this much, why not work for myself?"

3. https://www.amazon.com/Not-Done-Yet-Confidence-Workplace-ebook/dp/B08QLBH2L3/ref=sr_1_1?crid=CVCFV68PBJJW&keywords=Not+done+yet+-+bonnie+marcus&qid=1641406218&sprefix=not+done+yet+-+bonnie+marcus%2Caps%2C142&sr=8-1

INSIGHTS INTO CONTINUING TO WORK

INTERVIEW WITH **VICTORIA WOODS**,

CHIEF INVESTMENT ADVISOR AND CEO OF CHAPPELWOOD FINANCIAL SERVICES, AUTHOR, AND RADIO SHOW HOST

https://nanmckayconnects.com/2020/08/victoria-woods-2/

Victoria Woods

Victoria Woods is the founder, CEO, and Chief Investment Advisor to millionaires at Chappelwood Financial Services. She is an advisory board member for a national $47.5 billion wealth management firm. The governor appointed her the commissioner for the Oklahoma Status of Women, and she is a board member for the state of Oklahoma Finance Board. She has been interviewed on the *Today Show*, among many others, and is referred to as the Financial Diva, renowned for her financial advice.

With our clients, we have found that people are working longer than they want to. We have some people who have retired at 55 for whatever reason. An average would be between 62 and 66, but we have so many people who love what they do, and they are good at what they do. They don't want to retire. They have plenty of money to retire. That's not a desire for them. At some point, I can flip a switch. I can go just sit and watch the grass grow if I want to. Or I can work until I drop dead. I'm good at what I do. I want to contribute. Do you remember back in the day when there used to be mandatory retirement? I remember hearing this when I was a teenager and feeling so bad that they were making people retire. It was like you are useless to the world after age sixty or sixty-five. And I would think, "I don't want to become useless, irrelevant." Now they're begging people who are good to stay around or do contract labor. A lot of my clients do contract labor. They can retire if they want, but they're so good. And if they do retire, I work with them about going back as contract labor. So now they can work whenever they want, however many days they want. And it's now on their terms, which they love. And they earn as much, if not more.

* * *

INTERVIEW WITH **THRESETTE BRIGGS**, FOUNDER AND CEO OF PERFORMANCE 3, LLC

https://nanmckayconnects.com/2020/06/thresette-briggs/

Thresette Briggs

Thresette Briggs has been called a voice for high performance as Chief Performance Officer of Performance 3, a national leadership and professional development firm. She has over twenty years as a thought leader, collaborating with leaders in over ten industries to provide services and products for achieving high-performance cultures, including keynotes, organizational learning initiatives, and initial in-group coaching. She patented her performance assessment approach.

I was that person in corporate America who was climbing the ladder. I was doing all those things. And I was making that six-figure income, and that is very hard to leave. There were some transitions in my life where I decided there was no way I was going to be my highest-performing self or to fulfill my purpose by being in that position. I'm not bashing corporate America at all. It was very good to me, and I met a lot of great people whom I'm still connected to. But it just was not going to allow me to do what I feel I was called to do. Money is a barrier. You must carefully plan before you make that leap or have a strong support system around you to do it. Sometimes the job just may not be a good fit. Unfortunately, as I reflect on it, I think it wasn't necessarily a good fit for me. But I jumped at it, because it was money, and I needed it. I thought, "Okay, I will make this work." But when it is somewhere we are not really supposed to be, and we are not called to do it, it does not really work. No matter how hard you try or want to do it.

* * *

Do you want to leave the corporate world? Are you retired and bored with what you are doing? Do you have a passion? Do you want to make a difference in lives? Do you want to make your own gold to replace or supplement your current income? Do you plan to do a side hustle? Are you feeling like if you don't start a business, you might not have another chance? Do you feel like you would be starting all over again?

INSIGHTS INTO MAKING THE BREAK WITH CORPORATE

INTERVIEW WITH **ROBIN BREWTON**,

FOUNDER AND CEO OF STRATEGY MOSAIC, LLC

https://nanmckayconnects.com/2022/01/how-to-pivot-into-entrepreneurship-without-fear-robin-brewton/

Robin Brewton

Figure out your passion and run toward it. Don't run away from your job just because you're miserable. I see so many people who grasp at something, the next get-rich-quick scheme, a multilevel marketing company, just to get out of the misery that they're in. It doesn't make them happy. It is not successful. Instead of running away from that situation, find your passion and run toward it. I believe that if you are following your passion, you are not going to fail. The happiness is a trade-off for you, even if you are making less money. I also believe if whatever you want to do is of value to others' success, income will find you. The financial fear does not immediately go away. I tell people to do it as a side hustle for a while until you have some revenue and are comfortable taking that leap.

* * *

INTERVIEW WITH **MICHELLE MOORE**, FOUNDER AND CEO OF ELLE RATE, THE NEW YELP FOR WOMEN

https://nanmckayconnects.com/2021/09/how-to-elevate-women-in-business-michelle-moore/

Michelle Moore

Michelle Moore is an entrepreneur who pivoted to business after spending years in senior corporate marketing. After fourteen years of running a jewelry business from home, she is again pivoting to create a convenient and enjoyable way for women to partner with businesses and nonprofits that are committed to championing women.

My advice is to plan on being realistic. Try not to act on impulse. Try to map out what you're bringing in versus what you might be lacking to be able to really pull this off. Try to put your expenses to that list, and then double it in terms of how much it is going to cost and how much time it's going to take. And that was the hardest thing I did not want to hear when people were saying that to me. But fortunately, I did. It did transpire to being the reality of it all. For me. I think the hardest thing for people, especially if they are working right now, is the thinking, "Okay, I've got my medical. I've got my 401(k). I have my salary. How can I give that up for something that is a total unknown? How do I do that?"

I would ask, "How strong is your passion for what it is you want to do?" If you can tap into the courage of your convictions, this is what you are here to do. For me, the deathbed regret is a strong deterrent to me giving up. When I'm feeling like I am hitting rough waters, I don't want to have regrets on my deathbed. I know that I know that I can do this. And I will do this. I have a vision, and I have all the steps drawn out as to how I am going to get to that vision. It is not a pipe dream. It is not a lark. I am going to do this, and the people who are going to help me along the way will appear. They have appeared, and they will continue to appear. And they will do that for you, too, if you have that force. And that conviction. You will attract the people who need to help you get where you need to be.

* * *

According to the Kauffman Foundation,[4] an organization that studies entrepreneurship, the age group starting the greatest number of new businesses is people between the ages of fifty-five and sixty-four. Perhaps the question should be "Why not?" Think of the experience you bring to the table that you have gained by making other people money. Think about not having other people judge how much you are worth through your salary increases. Make that money for yourself! According to an article on Bustle.com,[5] statistics show that career women over fifty are more independent and are used to minimal work-life balance. They are less dependent on men for their happiness than prior generations and are more inclined to retain their independence and self-reliance. As a result, they are more likely to start searching for a work-life balance. They are not willing to give up the lifestyle afforded by their finances. You can create your own world by fulfilling your passion to create a profitable business that also satisfies your work-life balance.

The secret to pivoting is that the pivot happens in stages. Little steps lead to massive results. Your parents told you that if you went to school and got a good job, you would have security. You went to school, and you earned your degree. You found your job and worked for many years.

---

4. Kauffman Foundation https://www.kauffman.org/currents/the-new-adventures-of-older-entrepreneurs/#:~:text=The%20new%20age%20of%20entrepreneurs,38%25.

5. Bustle.com https://www.bustle.com/p/we-asked-283-millennial-women-about-work-life-balance-heres-what-they-said-15546142

You learned how to save money, and now you can learn how to create money. You can learn how to serve people through your own customer base.

Feeling the need to change has no age limit. The awakening to start something new is becoming a need rather than a want. Instead of a complete switch to another job, the answer may be a side hustle to bridge from one source to another. Or the solution may include going back to school. Or becoming an entrepreneur. And what would that take? What would you do? How can you decide what you are good at and what interests you? Those decisions can take a long, circuitous route. Give yourself the gift of finding out who you are at this stage and who you want to be. If you picked up this book, you know you want to be independent for as long as you physically and mentally can. You do not want to have to depend on your family, either to take money from them or to live with them because you cannot afford anything else.

The Pew Research Center estimates that by 2030 all baby boomers will be sixty-five or older. Ten thousand baby boomers turn sixty-five every day.[6] Baby boomers have changed the face of the U.S. population for more than seventy years and will continue to do so as more enter their senior years, a demographic shift often referred to as a "gray tsunami" (another stereotype.) The Pew Research Center estimates the baby boomer generation numbers about 73 million, and according to a Pew Research Center analysis of monthly labor force data, in 2019 the number of retired boomers increased more than in prior years.[7] Fifty-eight percent plan to continue working after they retire. Forty-three percent plan to work past age seventy or do not plan to retire. Boomers spend the most significant share of their money on education, mortgage debt, and health care. Thus, we may be able to conclude that,

6. Pew Research Center https://www.pewresearch.org/topic/generations-age/generations/baby-boomers/

7. https://www.pewresearch.org/fact-tank/2020/11/09/the-pace-of-boomer-retirements-has-accelerated-in-the-past-year/

although many boomers may not be able to buy their way out of old age, they can enjoy their old age as they go along.

Retirement sings its siren song, especially for career women tired of the grind and the emotional roller coaster. Retirement means different things to different people. To some people, retirement means that your time is spent playing golf, shopping, and having lunch with friends. For some, retirement means working at some endeavor, whether the work is volunteer or paid. You may have been an executive, but after retiring you are cleaning out dog pens at the local animal shelter and loving it. Neither option is right or wrong. Retirement is whatever makes you happy.

Perhaps you have already retired from your career. You have had that longed-for cup of coffee at 10 a.m. in your nightgown and enjoyed it. You have traveled and volunteered, and now you would like to supplement your income. You are searching for fulfillment and an elusive something to get your juices flowing again. You would like to do something creative and exciting where you are in control.

INSIGHTS ON "RETIREMENT"

INTERVIEW WITH **ESTHER WOJCICKI**,

BEST-SELLING AUTHOR OF
HOW TO RAISE SUCCESSFUL PEOPLE

https://nanmckayconnects.com/2021/08/how-to-empower-kids-and-the-world-esther-wojcicki/

Esther Wojcicki

Esther Wojcicki is famous for three things: teaching a high school class that has changed the lives of thousands of kids, inspiring Silicon Valley legends like Steve Jobs, and raising three daughters, each of whom have become famously successful.

So many people retire, but they don't just quit physically. They retire mentally. And that's such a waste. So many people with so much wisdom and so many skills. Why shouldn't you withdraw physically and mentally? What else should you do? You can help and work with others. First, it will help all those other people. But secondly, personally, for you, you will thrive and live a much better life. Research shows that one of the worst things you can do to yourself is to lose interest in what you're doing in life. It results in a lot of problems—psychological, physical, mental. It is so important to keep your physical and mental persona up if you can. I'm not retiring anytime soon. I'm happy to say I failed at retirement.

* * *

If you are in your fifties, sixties, or seventies, you may have quite a few years left that you can still work. And if you are in your eighties, you may prefer spending your time doing what you like to do, rather than just working at a job. The combination of work and age has no relevance or limits. Life expectancy is longest in Hong Kong or Japan at an average age of 85–88 for women and 82 for men. The United States ranks forty-sixth in life expectancy, at an average age of 79–81 for women and 76 for men. And many are outliving those ages. If you choose a career you like, you may find you get more satisfaction during retirement than in the career you worked during most of your life. In a 2012 *Parade* survey, 61 percent said they would not choose the same career.[8] Most people put more time and energy into finding the right car to buy than finding which career brings them the most satisfaction.

---

8. Parade source https://www.freemoneyfinance.com/2011/01/would-you-choose-the-same-career-again.html

INSIGHTS ON RETIREMENT CHOICES

INTERVIEW WITH **GINA GOREE HITCHENS**,

FOUNDER AND CEO OF GHG FINANCIAL PLANNING

https://nanmckayconnects.com/2021/04/how-to-approach-your-retirement-with-added-confidence-gina-goree-hitchens/

Gina Goree Hitchens

Gina Goree Hitchens is a seasoned financial professional, a vibrant lecturer, workshop facilitator, and presenter of financial education. She is the founder and CEO of GHG Financial Planning. As a Retirement Income Certified Professional, Gina helps retirees and near-retirees develop plans that create legacies through wealth protection strategies.

You have a sense of having a life of choice. If I choose to get up and work nine to five, fine. I don't think very many people would choose to be sixty-five, seventy, or seventy-five years old and going to work. But if they are developing their passion and doing what they're most called to do, you could work until seventy-five or eighty or whatever that age is. But that business comes down to your choice and connecting with your passion. You can set a financial goal and have a retirement plan to retire. You are your boss. At that point, you might like to create a lifestyle. This is what I want to do to connect with my passion. Rejoice—rejoice just finding and connecting to that life calling. I'm all about creating a life designed by dignity, independence, and choice. Whatever that means for you.

* * *

As we begin to dream, we think about what we want to do with our lives—the rest of our lives. We start to think about our passions, and we begin to analyze our current situations to see if they measure up. Sadly, where we are today often falls short.

The choice of becoming the boss in your world is a freeing experience. Making your own gold, you define everything, and you are in charge. Think of entrepreneurship as a new life—being reborn with a purpose and worth—a new beginning that will give you much of what you are missing or starting to feel is slipping away. You have a tremendous amount of experience to offer, and you can see years of fulfillment ahead because you get to be who you want to be. You feel good—sure, older, but good. And age becomes a plus, not a minus. No one says you must retire to do nothing. Now it's time to refire. Own your future. The two secrets for your success are entrepreneurial spirit and resilience. You have the opportunity to launch your venture—write your future—and control your destiny.

No longer are we chained to money or even a specific place. We have choices on what we do and where we live.

We must throw our shoulders back and appreciate who we are. You are a woman who has put some miles on her odometer, yes. However, instead of looking at them as miles, look at them as experience with the confidence that you know what you know. March with singer Helen Reddy and shout, "I am woman!" Own it. Celebrate it. And know that you can achieve even more than you have already. Whatever the age on your birth certificate, that age is the right age for you and the right time for you to climb another mountain, ford another stream, follow another rainbow because you have a dream.

ACTION STEP 1.

MY ROAD TO FREEDOM, FLEXIBILITY, AND FINANCIAL INDEPENDENCE

Check your current category.

- ☐ I am under age 50.
- ☐ I am age 50-60.
- ☐ I am age 61-70.
- ☐ I am age 71-80.
- ☐ I am age 81-90.
- ☐ I am not any of these ages.
- ☐ I am currently working.
- ☐ I currently own a business.
- ☐ I will retire in the next five years.
- ☐ I am currently retired.

What do you see in your vision looking forward?

____

____

Why do you want to move toward a new horizon?

____

____

What might the second act look like?

____

____

Describe the freedom this would bring to you.

____

____

How will this move bring you recognition for your hard work?

____

____

CHAPTER 1 TAKEAWAYS

IMAGINE YOUR WORLD OF FULFILLMENT AND FREEDOM

- The S.O.A.R. Launch and Growth Plan for successful entrepreneurship, women over fifty.
- Questions to ask yourself if you want to pivot and start a business you are passionate about.
- Being over fifty and the opportunities you have.
- Gendered ageism experienced by women over fifty at the workplace.
- Being underestimated as a woman—the work-life balance debate.
- Continuing to work—retiring and refiring.
- Making the break with corporate—is your passion strong enough?
- Retirement—what to do in retirement.
- Retirement choices—this is the time to own your future as a strong woman.

CHAPTER 2

CREATE A MINDSET FOR AN EFFECTIVE AND EXCITING LIFE

Amid the concerns of women's futures after the pandemic, many women today are rising like phoenixes out of the ashes and making an impact on legislation, climate change, finance, the boardroom, technology, and education. You can be that person who makes a difference in the world. The clock is ticking, but the clock is propelling you forward into a future that beckons with determination and diligence, not fairy dust and magic. Make life better for future generations by stepping into your power.

INSIGHTS ON SUCCEEDING

INTERVIEW WITH **CATHERINE CROSSLIN**,

FOUNDER AND CEO OF INSTAR PERFORMANCE

https://nanmckayconnects.com/2021/05/how-to-be-the-maker-of-champions-catherine-crosslin/

Catherine Crosslin

Starting out as a basketball coach, **Cat Crosslin** transitioned to her own leadership development company. She is referred to as "the maker of champions."

Your mind is picture-seeking. We tend to think that we are focusing consciously. Understand that you are focusing on the clearest picture you have, whether that picture is good for you or not. The clearest picture always wins. That might be a clear picture of what you are most afraid of or most insecure about. Or the visual could be a clear picture of your home on the beach in Maui, where you hear the waves crashing, and you have this clear picture of the dreams you have in life. Focus is everything. Make sure you are focusing on what you really want instead of what you don't want.

* * *

Ask yourself two questions, first: "What is the best possible outcome?" Maybe the best possible outcome is that you get off the hamster wheel that goes round and round and become your true, self-actualizing self? What would that look like? And the second question is, "What is the outcome if I don't pivot?" Where will your life be in three years or five years? Timing is everything, and the time has to be right for you. However, as the famous saying goes, "If not now, when?"

INSIGHTS ON SUCCEEDING

INTERVIEW WITH **ROBIN BREWTON**,

FOUNDER AND CEO OF STRATEGY MOSAIC, LLC

https://nanmckayconnects.com/2022/01/how-to-pivot-into-entrepreneurship-without-fear-robin-brewton/

Robin Brewton

I think women are afraid of failure. There's a poem out there I have read, I don't know how many times. It is called "What If I Fail?" by Erin Hanson, and it is literally five little lines:

There is freedom waiting for you,
On the breezes of the sky,
And you ask, "What if I fail?"
Oh but my darling,
What if you fly?

* * *

INSIGHTS ON ADVOCATING FOR YOURSELF

Advocating for yourself is essential in your business. One of the best ways to overcome your fears and doubts is positive self-talk. Positive self-talk is a lifesaver when you start beating yourself up or you start having negative thoughts, like "I don't know enough to create a business plan. I'm too old to learn how social media works." We all have those thoughts when we approach a new and daunting task or a new event, and especially if we think we are going to be judged. Positive self-talk creates an inner monologue that makes you feel good about yourself and everything going on in your life. It is an optimistic voice in your head that encourages you to look at the bright side, pick yourself up when you fall, and recognize when you fail.

Self-talk can be both positive and negative. Positive self-talk can empower and encourage your optimistic side. Negative self-talk can limit you to the point of feeling so unsure that you are unable to deal with the situation. Positive self-talk can override negative self-talk and help you be a more positive person, and the positive self-talk may even have a positive influence on your health.

Recognizing when negative self-talk is taking over your mind, along with affecting decision-making, will create an awareness that will allow your positive self-talk to take over so you can power through the situations and decisions that are limiting your positive behavior. As an entrepreneur, you will face heavy decisions. If your negative self-talk is allowed to take over, you may feel frozen in place. Identify when negative behavior starts—for example, when you are blaming yourself for everything or you are magnifying the negative aspects of a situation where your life seems negative, and nothing is positive. If you tend to expect the worst, instead of the best, the negative thoughts can immediately set your course of action. If everything is on one end of the spectrum or the other consistently, the gray area in between will be difficult to view.

If you have been in the regular working world for a long time, just the thought of starting a business may seem like an enormous challenge. In taking that next step toward doing something else, which may seem like a leap instead of a step, you may be encountering the fear monster that starts in your gut and says, “Why would you do something else? What do you know? What makes you think your experience and skills are worthy?” You picture the fear monster pointing at you, saying, “You aren’t the expert. You are not a star in this industry.” These thoughts are perfectly normal.

The little voice in our head also says, “Let’s just stay where we are. Let’s not take the risk.” That little voice can stop you and can stop your opportunity. Instead, tell yourself, “I can do anything I decide to do.” Don’t take no for an answer. Don’t let the little voice win. Stay open-minded.

Sometimes fear and insecurity are rooted in the past and continue to be an influence on doubting your decisions. The imposter syndrome is very common among many high-performing people who sometimes feel like they do not deserve what they have and fear that they will be exposed as frauds. In interviewing trailblazing women, two stories stand out in my mind. The stories of these women demonstrate how to recognize the root of the struggle to overcome your negative thoughts and, instead, how you can take control, kick the monster to the ground, and stomp on him—removing all doubt of your ability to succeed!

INSIGHTS ON BEATING THE IMPOSTER SYNDROME

INTERVIEW WITH **BRIANNA MCDONALD**,

PRESIDENT OF THE NORTHWEST REGION OF THE KEIRETSU FORUM

https://nanmckayconnects.com/2021/04/invest-in-and-support-women-brianna-mcdonald/

Brianna McDonald

Brianna McDonald is president of the Northwest & Rockies Region of the Keiretsu Forum investor network, the largest and most active venture investor globally, comprising over fifty chapters with over 3,000 active members investing more than $450 million into over 600 companies.

I have spent most of my life overcoming internal barriers that I created from what I had learned in my early childhood. My parents relocated to a new city when I was seven years old. Upon leaving that city and starting a new one at a new school, I had a very difficult time acclimating into that new environment. As a result, I dealt with a tremendous amount of bullying over seven years. It was pretty extreme, different cases and scenarios. In the '80s, bullying was dealt with a lot differently than it is today. What ended up happening was my parents ended up leaving the state that they grew up in and relocating to a different city to provide me a new start.

There was a lot of name-calling and making fun of me, a lot of exclusion. There was physical abuse that also occurred. My mom tells me stories. I don't remember a lot of it. I've blocked it out of my mind. I walked a mile to and from school because they didn't have bus service. I know that sounds really old-fashioned, but they did that in the '80s. On the way home, some kids ripped a necklace off me. One person there was a boy I liked, and they played a joke saying that he liked me. Two days later, I found out that it was a complete joke. Things like that. Then the culprits were five girls who held me underwater in a lake while I was playing a game with some friends, and that was the straw that broke the camel's back.

It affects me still every day when I go out into the world, but what I really encourage people to do is to overcome their own obstacles. I'm really good at dishing out suggestions to people and talking about my story. When it comes to me following my own suggestions, some of the time that's a little bit more difficult. I deal with the imposter syndrome daily, especially working in an industry that is dominated by men. But I show up unapologetically and go do what I need to do. I support entrepreneurs and my investors. I usually go home and, with the confidence of my few good friends, talk with them, and they help me get over different things I'm dealing with. Is it self-doubt? Is it fear? Some of it is self-doubt; some of it is that I don't think I deserve what I have. It's funny. I do a lot of ruminating on "I shouldn't have said that" type of talk in my mind. I'm not politically correct at all. I talk like a sailor. I'm really honest. I'm very opinionated about certain things. Sometimes, I don't fit that mold of what you should look like as a woman business leader, and I approach it a little bit differently. I think that because I don't fit into one of those boxes, it affects me in different ways.

Imposter syndrome is really fascinating. It's basically like you, your mind, and the self-talk that you have, that you're not actually supposed to be in that spot. Especially as entrepreneurs are going out there, achieving these different goals and milestones. They're running that marathon to build their company, but they think they shouldn't be the one doing it. It should be somebody else. It's the self-talk monologue that you're not the person to do it. It's an interesting mindset. It's a lot of overcoming not identifying it and identifying it when it can be useful. I don't necessarily think imposter syndrome is always a negative thing. There are always things that can be learned. And I'm very introspective in that way of finding how I can always do better. Understand where those touch points come in, when that imposter syndrome would be creeping in, identify them, not judge them, recognize them, and then continue moving forward.

It gives me the ability to really understand people and who people are. There are a lot of individuals and a lot of leaders out there making decisions for many different people, especially in government, as we deal with homelessness or drug abuse or other issues. And none of them have walked in their shoes, and what goes on in that mindset, and what it is to overcome what they are dealing with. I think it gives me a good sense of people and being able to read people, understand different challenges they're facing, or how I can help. I think it gives me an inner strength. Absolutely, yeah, I do deal with more things that are adverse, because I have been through it.

* * *

INSIGHTS ON "HELL, I'M STILL HERE!"

INTERVIEW WITH **MARLENE WAGMAN-GELLER**,

AUTHOR OF BOOKS ON WOMEN EMPOWERMENT

https://nanmckayconnects.com/2021/06/how-to-empower-women-through-books-marlene-wagman-geller/

Marlene Wagman-Geller

Marlene Wagman-Geller is the author of ten books, half of which celebrate the greatness of women.

I hope I've made a difference in people's lives because the common denominator for my books has been "Don't succumb to the problems, keep your eye on the prize, and capture the power of persistence." If I can get that message across, then I hope I have made a difference. Initially, I was an accidental activist for feminism because my first book on the topic of feminism was **Still I Rise**. *I met a woman. Our paths should never otherwise have crossed because we had such different lives. She told me so many stories that I realized everything that could go wrong in her life, did. I remember, I wanted to give solace, but the only thing I could think of was, "I'm sorry." I remember she said to me, "Hell, I'm still here." That meeting made me realize, here is this woman who life has knocked in the teeth. And yet, she says, "Hell, I'm still here." I thought that if I can write a book that will showcase women who, no matter how much trouble they had, they keep saying, "Hell, I'm still here," maybe the readers could gain from that as well.*

* * *

As these stories demonstrate, the influencer may be an ongoing series of events, or the influencer may be a significant emotional event that can interrupt or override your choices and set the trajectory for the rest of your life. Dr. Morris Massey[9] first described a significant emotional event as a standout experience or event that has shaped you. The significant emotional event disrupts you on a physical, emotional, and mental level so you think or behave differently in the future. Dr. Massey's definition is "an experience that is so mentally arresting the experience becomes a catalyst for you to consider, examine, and possibly change your initial values or value system."

INSIGHTS ON THE INFLUENCE OF SIGNIFICANT EMOTIONAL EVENTS

NAN MCKAY, PRESIDENT

NAN MCKAY AND ASSOCIATES AND
FOUNDER AND CEO, NAN MCKAY CONNECTS, LLC

https://nanmckayconnects.com/about

Nan McKay

For me, that significant emotional event occurred at age eleven. We went from an above-average lifestyle to being the pariah in a small town of 3,000 people. My high-living father was killed in a car accident, along with three other people. He had newly purchased a Jaguar, a fast sports car, and was giving a ride to the son of a prominent family. We discovered he was a gambler when many people called us asking for their money. Because we were the relatives left, we paid for his last act. My brother was six and my sister was three months old.

9. https://en.wikipedia.org/wiki/Morris_Massey. https://adflorem.com/blog/my-significant-emotional-event/#:~:text=Dr%20Massey%20defines%20a%20Significant,initial%20values%20or%20value%20system.%E2%80%9D

My mother had not worked for many years, but now she was responsible for the care of three children, with no job and no money. She vowed she would not leave the small town until she reimbursed everyone he owed. Pretty brave for a homemaker, especially when no one appreciated her efforts. But what to do? No jobs were available in the tiny town, and she had no experience. She went to work at a bar and restaurant on the outskirts of town until about 2 a.m. The job allowed her to take care of my sister during the day while I was at school, and my responsibility after she left for work was to take care of the kids.

Several of the boys in the community knew that my mother was gone at night and, probably because their parents had unkind things to say about us, they thought we would be a good target. They drove by at night, shining their spotlight into our living room. They threw dirt at the windows in the kitchen. But the worst was still to come. One night I heard voices in the basement and feet pounding on the back staircase from the basement to the kitchen door. I grabbed my sister and brother and ran into the tiny bathroom in the house, the only room in the house that locked. Both kids were crying, and I tried to hush them because I didn't want to give our hiding place away. But unfortunately, all I remember is boys shouting and banging on the bathroom door, which I was sure would break. My heart doesn't pound anymore when I think of it, but I can feel the fear creeping into my chest when the dark sets in, and I am alone. My imagination runs wild.

That incident must have been the deciding factor because my mother quit her job. But again, what to do to make money? All we had was a small Social Security payment and the rent from the upstairs, which was not enough to sustain a household of four people. My mother was artistic, and she decided to start a business. She bought a hearse and picked up store dummies (mannequins) from department stores. The year was 1952. We had a one-stall detached garage, and my mother hung the mannequins upside down in the garage to spray-paint them. Then she painted faces on them, and her friend Evelyn, who had a beauty shop in her home, restyled the wigs. We had many near-accidents with naked women hanging upside down since the garage doors were left open because of the fumes from the paint.

Finally, the mannequins throughout the area were all spiffed up, and my mother decided to focus on dolls. She painted a room in our basement and opened a doll shop and hospital. The newspaper published an article on the business, and people came from miles around to drop off their dolls for refurbishing. The antique dolls needed restringing, rewigging, and repainting. She and Evelyn did it all. She eventually opened a store in the town center and sold new dolls and clothes as well. Her mantra was, "Never rely on your husband to make a living. Always be able to support yourself."

* * *

After attending many self-help conferences, I recognized that I had choices, stamina, determination, and a clear choice. The mantra of "Everything I need is within me now" is part of my positive self-talk. If you feel this way, you are not alone. Many free programs are available on YouTube or from other sources from people like Kim Walsh Phillips, Ryan Levesque, Russell Brunson, Dean Graziosi, and Tony Robbins. I have attended many of their programs, and each one has helped me in taking those small pivot steps. We need a mix of inspiration, motivation, strategy, and tactics.

The women I have interviewed on TrailBlazers Impact Interviews are some of the bravest women I know. They have climbed mountains, overcome hurdles, and they are still racing to the finish line. They have risen above their beginnings, the stories in their heads, and have come out the other side to say, "Enough! You don't own me anymore!" The self-doubt does not entirely go away. Successful women continue to hear the cautionary negative voices in their head, but they have learned the art of positive self-talk.

The key is to learn how to turn negative self-talk into positive self-talk. When you constantly reinforce the positive self-talk, the positive self-talk becomes normal for you, and the voice in your head starts to go directly to that point. Pinpoint situations or experiences where negative self-talk is most likely to occur. If you can anticipate what has happened in the past in those experiences, you can prepare to shift to the positive self-talk quickly.

Humor is a great antidote for negative self-talk. "Am I taking myself or the situation too seriously? Am I going on automatic pilot into negative self-talk?" Deal with the potentially negative environment by laughing at yourself and saying, "I'm doing the talk again. I'm falling into the trap." Have a substitute positive statement ready to counterbalance that little negative voice. Cut yourself some slack.

Let me give you an example. I have given thousands of speeches and seminars. Prior to the talk, a little voice starts by saying, "Uh-oh. Watch out. This time the talk may be bad." I have learned to tamp the negative talk down and replace that talk with, "You will do fabulously well. Your talk will be a wild success, better than you can ever imagine." Somehow, that positive self-talk calms me and points me in the right direction.

Switching from a negative thought to a positive thought simply takes awareness and practice. Look for inspiring images or words to replace any negative thoughts that start to surface. Surround yourself with positive people and listen to how they express their outlook on life. Be aware of when you start to fall into the negative self-talk thoughts. Find uplifting quotations and post little reminders around your office or home. One I have posted on my printer is, "You have to fight through the bad days to earn the best days of your life." Read and listen to stories about people who have overcome adversities. You may realize your challenges are far less than theirs were. They did it. So can you!

What helps an entrepreneur more than anything is optimism. That mindset creates an energy that drives action. If you look on the bright side and see possibilities, your problem-solving will be easier.

ACTION STEP 2.

SHIFT YOUR BELIEFS

Review the pairs of beliefs. Choose the belief you now hold. If it is a limiting negative belief, develop the skills to flip to the positive thought.

- ☐ **Negative:** I'm too old to start over.
- ☐ **Positive:** My miles of experience will provide me with a leg up immediately.

- ☐ **Negative:** I will disappoint everyone if I change my mind.
- ☐ **Positive:** I have the power to make a different decision and others will understand.

- ☐ **Negative:** I need to look young to be acknowledged.
- ☐ **Positive:** Age equals experience in the business world and is admired. I have the experience.

- ☐ **Negative:** I am not the expert.
- ☐ **Positive:** I haven't had exactly this experience, but I am a great learner.

- ☐ **Negative:** I am not well-known in an industry.
- ☐ **Positive:** I am excited about becoming well known in a new industry.

☐ **Negative:** I have no power over my future.

☐ **Positive:** I have a whole new life ahead of me!

☐ **Negative:** I've never had my own business before.

☐ **Positive:** A business is a wonderful opportunity to learn from others and grow.

☐ **Negative:** This won't work.

☐ **Positive:** I can and will give it my all to make it work.

☐ **Negative:** I am not ready for a pivot because it is one giant leap.

☐ **Positive:** I can take smaller steps to a new, exciting outcome.

☐ **Negative:** ____________________

☐ **Positive:** ____________________

☐ **Negative:** ____________________

☐ **Positive:** ____________________

☐ **Negative:** ____________________

☐ **Positive:** ____________________

Role models boost motivation by modeling a guide to achieving success. On TrailBlazers Impact Interviews, the women interviewed tell their stories, illustrating how they overcame their challenging obstacles. Typical characteristics of ordinary women with extraordinary achievements include a clear sense of values, a commitment to community, and an acceptance of others. Almost all of the people interviewed had a positive outlook on life, providing inspiration to others to uncover their weakness and realize their potential to achieve success. Their own role models were often family members. People who overcame adversity often used that adversity to fuel their motivation to succeed.

INSIGHT ON FAMILY ROLE MODEL INFLUENCE

INTERVIEW WITH **LAURA YAMANAKA**,

FOUNDER AND CEO OF TEAMCFO

https://nanmckayconnects.com/2020/07/laura-yamanaka/

Laura Yamanaka

As President and co-owner of teamCFO, **Laura Yamanaka** and her employees partner with startups and small to midsize businesses to improve company performance and growth. Yamanaka leads and supports women in business as past president of the National Association of Women Business Owners (NAWBO). She is also the chair of the National Institute, the NAWBO foundation.

The biggest influencer in my family was probably my great-grandmother, but I never spoke to her about this. My great-grandmother was an immigrant. She came from Japan, emigrated to Hawaii with her husband, and they had nothing. And back then women had children and kept the house cleaned and had babies. They had five kids and my grandfather passed away. My grandmother was young. She was in her early thirties, with five kids, and no skill set. All she knew to do was cook. She would make lunches for the field hands and would carry the meals to them by hand.

Then she got a little bit of money, and she got a wheelbarrow. And she would make those lunches and carry them out to the fields in a wheelbarrow.

Then she saved up her money and got a little hand truck. She saved up more money and got a truck. She saved up more money and finally had a brick-and-mortar highly successful business. That business still operates on Maui today.

That experience reinforced to her that it is important that girls have the same opportunity to have a skill set just in case something happened. I remember it being drilled into my head by my mom: "You have to be able to support yourself. Fine, get married, have a husband, but life is fickle," as my great-grandmother learned.

My mother made sure all of her daughters were trained. One was a court reporter—very progressive for those days. I find myself saying the same things to my daughters: "Have a career and support yourself." It's my great-grandmother's words coming out. Even though she had no idea what an accountant did, I'm sure the way she kept her money in a coffee can was her accounting system. It worked for her.

I believe she was the one who put me on the path of realizing that I needed to be able to support myself. And along the way I learned that, yes, I have to support myself, but I might as well make a difference while I'm doing it. And I wanted to be good at it. And I figured out very early on that when you're good at something, you can make money doing it. There's no harm in enjoying what you do and making money at the same time.

* * *

INTERVIEW WITH **IRIS ANN COOPER**,

FOUNDER AND CEO OF GLORY FOODS,
TRADED ON THE STOCK MARKET

https://nanmckayconnects.com/2020/06/dr-iris-ann-cooper/.

Iris Ann Cooper

Iris Ann Cooper became cofounder of the first line of packaged ethnic foods found on grocery stores across the nation, under the brand name Glory Foods. Over time, she was able to take the company public with an Initial Public Offering (IPO) that grew the company its place on the New York Stock Exchange as GLYYY. As a young black woman from Indiana, she encountered many incidences of discrimination based on both race and gender but never allowed such encounters to derail her dreams, or her potential!

I grew up with the philosophy that you do not put all your eggs in one basket—that you don't take on that kind of risk for your bread and butter every day. When I began to ask for money, the response was, we are going to provide food and clothing for you. You are going to be at school every day; you will have everything you need. But if you want money to go to the movies or to hang out with your friends, that's on you.

I began to babysit. I began to start lemonade and cookie stands. I did what I could think of, anything I could think of, so that I didn't have to go through that dialogue with my mom or my dad like "What have you done lately to bring some food into this house?" That's how my brother and I were brought up. We were contributors to the household, basically to ourselves. All through, I'd say beginning in the seventh or eighth grade, all the way through high school, we had jobs or had businesses. My father had a part-time business. My mom was the first African American Avon lady in Evansville, Indiana. That was her side hustle when she was a social worker by day. I grew up in that environment.

* * *

To more fully understand the gifts you bring to the table, consider life mapping, a visual representation of a person's life. A life map can include anything that has meaning to the owner, such as key life events, emotions, people, goals, and dreams. People use life maps to gain self-knowledge, set personal objectives, or just for fun. People use life mapping to understand their unique gifts, giving them the insight to lead authentic lives. Seeing your personal journey mapped out helps you realize which ups and downs most affected your journey and allows you to appreciate your specialness and perhaps celebrate that you are still standing!

INSIGHTS ON LIFE MAPPING

INTERVIEW WITH **MONIKA K. MOSS-GRANSBERRY**,

ENTREPRENEUR, BUSINESS COACH, AUTHOR, ORGANIZATIONAL CONSULTANT, AND FOUNDER OF MKM MANAGEMENT CONSULTING

https://nanmckayconnects.com/2021/06/how-to-transform-your-organization-monika-moss-gransberry/

Monika K. Moss-Gransberry

Monika K. Moss-Gransberry is a best-selling author, a self-mastery coach, and an organizational consultant. She serves as president and CEO of MKM Management Consulting. She has dedicated her talents to helping organizations and individuals create powerful roadmaps to their vision.

We do a life-mapping session on mapping out people's third act. As we embrace our elderhood, we're still vital. We're still happy; we're still able to do a lot of things. And we don't want to work so hard. And we want a little more fun in our lives. Can you visualize that scenario? What is it that you can create for yourself that you can sustain over time as you age?

In their mid-career, women start saying, "I like this; I don't like that. This event is fulfilling; this is not fulfilling. How can I go to the next level? How can I create a better lifestyle, even if it's not a career change? How do I recalibrate to take as much care of myself as I do others?" Especially as women, we do a lot of that with everybody else first.

Sharing and growing together around different aha moments, having some structure by which to start to sort out the learning that we are getting as living human beings, from our experiences, and claiming the things that we want, that is what will bring us joy and happiness and security and safety and all the things that are important to us, really figuring out what is essential. And how I want to live my life.

* * *

Have you reached the conclusion that, although your skin was tighter and your hips were narrower, the first act was okay, but the second act coming up is going to be beyond okay if you make the decision to make your second act fabulous? Use your courage and fortitude to complete the action steps in this book, and you will find the decision starts to crystalize itself.

If I asked whether you grew up thinking you wanted to be an entrepreneur, most people would answer no. The exception might be if your parent was an entrepreneur and you saw him or her as a role model. However, sometimes people in their early twenties want to start a business. The question is, why? Are they looking for independence? Do they think they will get rich quickly? Does the business idea hold the freedom they are craving?

INSIGHTS ON DECIDING TO BE AN ENTREPRENEUR

INTERVIEW WITH **SUSAN MCPHERSON**,

FOUNDER AND CEO OF MCPHERSON STRATEGIES
AND AUTHOR OF *THE LOST ART OF CONNECTING*

https://nanmckayconnects.com/2021/07/how-to-build-meaningful-connections-susan-mcpherson/

Susan McPherson

Susan McPherson is a serial connector, seasoned communicator, and author of *The Lost Art of Connecting.* She's also the founder and CEO of McPherson Strategies, a communications consultancy focused on the intersection of brands and social impact. McPherson shifted from the corporate world in 2013 and started her own business without any hope of succeeding long-term. She was named one of fifty women over fifty who are leading the way by *Forbes.*

> *I did not have a burning desire to be an entrepreneur in my twenties, thirties, even most of my forties. I often credit myself as an accidental entrepreneur. I had worked in corporate America for many, many years and kept hitting the glass ceiling, like many of us who came of age professionally in the late 1980s and '90s. And then it became apparent that if I was going to continue to grow, I may just have to put my own flag out the door. And now,*

almost eight years later, we are very profitable, very happy, and doing important social impact work.

* * *

In interviewing people for my TrailBlazers Impact podcast and video business, I always want to know, "What is the story behind the story?" How did they get from where they were to where they are now? What was the spark that channeled them in the direction of entrepreneurship? Why? Because they usually did not start out thinking they wanted entrepreneurship as a career. What brought them to this point? Was it a set of circumstances that brought them to this decision?

Entrepreneurs are a different breed of cat. They have a tiny spark that grows into a full-blown passion. To sustain a business long-term, you will have to draw on that passion.

Entrepreneurship isn't for everyone. If you are currently working in a job-job, a career job, and you want to be an entrepreneur, assess whether entrepreneurship is for you. Many people think, "I'd like to be my own boss." I've even heard "I want more free time." Entrepreneurship is a different path than a career job, where someone else is paying you. You may not even realize the freedom and luxuries you have had in that job. Some of the job perks might include checking your texts every time one comes in, engaging in social communication, going home at night with time on your own, taking time off for vacation or sick leave, and attending your child's teacher conference or birthday party. When you dive into entrepreneurship, you will redefine the word "critical," and that assessment will guide your actions.

Your life as an entrepreneur is rarely dull and boring. You are not sitting at your desk, watching the clock, and wishing time would go faster. It's the opposite. You are always wishing you had more time in the day.

You are keeping balls in the air and, if anything, your ability to focus is sometimes difficult because so much is going on around you all the time.

You feel like you are constantly growing, but you are challenging yourself to learn new skills, a new app, a new tool that will help your business grow. Endless courses and offers to learn something new are available. Instead of waiting for the company you work for to suggest you take a course, you proactively can decide whether to take a course or not. Of course, the difference is that you pay for the course. However, the expenditure is deductible.

Entrepreneurship on a continuum has responsibility on one end and flexibility on the other end, with everything else in between. Especially in a small business, you have complete control and responsibility over anything and everything that happens in your business. You don't have to go to a boss or a board for a decision. Therefore, you are not complacent or waiting for someone else to take action. It's your decision. It's your action.

The best entrepreneurs know that they must get through the tough times, and that takes perseverance and grit. Picture a dog on a very tasty bone. The dog will stay on that bone until the bone is either finished or down to a manageable size. The dog is you as an entrepreneur. Your grit, your tenacity, your determination are what will get you through the hard parts.

INSIGHTS ON GRIT

INTERVIEW WITH **SHANNON HUFFMAN POLSON**,

FOUNDER AND CEO OF THE GRIT INSTITUTE AND AUTHOR OF *THE GRIT FACTOR: COURAGE, RESILIENCE, AND LEADERSHIP IN THE MOST MALE-DOMINATED ORGANIZATION IN THE WORLD* AND *NORTH OF HOPE: A DAUGHTER'S ARCTIC JOURNEY*

https://nanmckayconnects.com/2020/09/shannon-polson/

Shannon Huffman Polson

Shannon Polson exemplifies the true meaning of grit: courage, tenacity, and perseverance. A native of Alaska, at age nineteen she became the youngest woman ever to climb Denali, the highest mountain in North America, and she went on to summit Mount Rainier and Mount Kilimanjaro. She raced long-course triathlons and took journeys to Alaska's Arctic. After graduating from Duke University, she entered the military, becoming one of the first women to fly the Apache attack helicopter in the U.S. Army. The Grit Institute is the culmination of five years of research into grit, including most notably the lessons, stories, and candid recommendations from outstanding military leaders.

> *One of the questions that I get asked by people for themselves, for their teams, and for their children is, "What can you do to build grit? Is grit something that you just have that you are just born with, or you aren't?" I think the answer is very clearly that all of us have access to grit. All of us can build grit by doing hard things. You do hard things by doing small things, and then slightly bigger, and then slightly bigger.*

I think that is absolutely the way that we do anything well. We must give ourselves permission because we are used to taking these giant leaps, to take some baby steps.

Just keep moving forward. It is just small steps forward right now, being gentle with ourselves and our people, always moving in the direction of whatever that intermediate goal is that may be shifting around, and always stay connected to that core purpose. It is something that I'm constantly working on as well. I get just as overwhelmed as anybody.

* * *

ACTION STEP 3.

GAIN A POSITIVE ENTREPRENEURIAL MINDSET

Describe one of your passions.

____

____

If you feel you have a mission in life, what is it?

____

____

What does success look like to you?

____

____

What is the story behind the story?

____

____

List any relatives who were entrepreneurs. Describe whether you feel you have entrepreneurship interest in common with them.

____

____

What actions will you take to turn your limiting, negative thoughts into positive self-talk?

____

____

What will be the benefits of entrepreneurship for you?

____

____

CHAPTER 2 TAKEAWAYS

CREATE A MINDSET FOR AN EFFECTIVE AND EXCITING LIFE

- Creating the mindset for an effective and exciting life—becoming a passionate and adventurous entrepreneur.
- How to succeed in business.
- Imposter syndrome—a firsthand experience.
- Overcoming the fear and not letting it manage you.
- "Hell, I'm still here!"—what event will shape the rest of your life?
- The influence of significant emotional events—turning negative self-talk into positive self-talk.
- Examples of how to flip negative talk into positive.
- Family role model influence—using a life map to identify special gifts.
- Life mapping—why do you want to become an entrepreneur?
- Deciding to be an entrepreneur—the ups and downs of becoming an entrepreneur.
- Grit—the art of doing smaller things first, before moving on to bigger things.

CHAPTER 3

VISUALIZE A BUSINESS DRIVING YOUR PASSION, PURPOSE, AND PROFIT

Visualize yourself in your new business with a cup of your favorite beverage beside your computer, with few interruptions. You are in control of your world. You may have decided on your business tentatively. We will help you crystalize what you want to do and then help you do it.

The concept of business is broader than previously defined. In the past, we had one model of entrepreneurship, which was work hard to attain and maintain profitability and get the business to the point of selling the business or handing the business off to your children. We have a new model of entrepreneurship—lifestyle entrepreneurship—which intrigued the millennials and is now spreading to the Gen Xers and even the baby boomers.

Lifestyle entrepreneurship is a new concept but is catching on and may be within your reach! This type of entrepreneurship focuses on having an income source that supports the lifestyle you really want. Lifestyle entrepreneurship has four components:

- **Time**—control your own agenda and schedule
- **Money**—having enough to enjoy the lifestyle you want
- **Control of the work itself**—doing things your way
- **Skills**—using skills you have but may not have using in your current job

Are you a social entrepreneur? A social entrepreneur is a person who pursues novel applications that have the potential to solve community-based problems. Social entrepreneurship is important because this model provides a framework for businesses to find their own success in the pursuit of helping others. These individuals are willing to take on the risk and effort to create positive changes in society through their initiatives.

Esther Wojcicki, a legendary educator, the Godmother of Silicon Valley, and author of the no. 1 Amazon bestseller *How to Raise Successful People*, has positively impacted the lives of thousands of children (including her own three successful daughters: the CEO of YouTube, the CEO and founder of 23andMe, and a top UCSF medical researcher). Wojcicki started thinking about this dilemma:

> *Too often, traditional education dims that bright light of curiosity. When success is measured by checking the right boxes, children—often the smartest and most creative among them—shut down. They can do the work, but the joy is gone. How can we end the passive screen time? How can we get kids engaged in their own education, excited to learn and not just putting in FaceTime?*

As a result, she created a peer-to-peer edutainment site at https://Tract.app.

What is the lifestyle you are looking for? Are you a candidate for lifestyle entrepreneurship or are you more of a traditional entrepreneur?

Lifestyle entrepreneurs, individuals who create businesses for the purpose of changing their lifestyles instead of making profits, usually want to create a business because they are passionate about the business concept and believe that the company will be personally rewarding for them. It does not mean the entrepreneur wants to choose a business that brings in no revenue. However, the revenue and profit are not the driving force.

If nothing else, the pandemic taught us that most of us can work from anywhere in the world. Yes, we may miss the personal interaction with people and, yes, some of us may feel "Zoomed out," but the reality is that many businesses—because of the internet—can operate effectively from anywhere in the world. For many businesses, as long as we have a laptop and a phone, we are business-mobile.

What does that mean? We can live anywhere. We are no longer geographically tied to a location. We can work at something because we love doing the business; we are passionate about it. Not because it's all that's offered in our little town. Not because we took on this career because our parents wanted us to do it. Not because of the guilt we feel because of the money spent on educating us. Not because this career decision was "the right thing to do" at the time. Not because you have done the business for most of your life. We are doing it because we love what we do, we are passionate about it, and we want our freedom!

Lifestyle entrepreneurs enjoy and place their emphasis on freedom as well as passion. They may want to work only enough to earn a specified income because their goal is to support their lifestyle. Lifestyle entrepreneurs are probably not as focused on growth as other entrepreneurs if they have enough to support their passions, interests, or hobbies.

Lifestyle businesses have more of a personal nature. Lifestyle businesses are directly tied to the skills or talent, energy, personality, and contacts of the founder of the business. As a lifestyle business founder, you may want to achieve a flexible schedule, remain in a geographic area for a family reason, or simply exercise your own freedom of expression. You are the driver with a strong personal involvement, which means investors are not usually involved with lifestyle businesses.

What's the difference between a traditional entrepreneur and a lifestyle entrepreneur? A traditional entrepreneur chooses a career and builds a life around the career. The home you buy, the people you associate with, the car you drive, the city you live in, the commute you take to work . . . the career is the driver. Nothing is wrong with this career except that if you don't love it, or do it strictly for the money, or if you dread getting up in the morning, just accepting what you are doing by banging on your alarm clock and reluctantly putting your feet from the bed to the floor. Then the business is much like a career working for someone else. Why take on the risk if you feel this way?

INSIGHTS ON TRADITIONAL VERSUS LIFESTYLE ENTREPRENEURSHIP

INTERVIEW WITH **JOANNA BLOOR**,

FOUNDER AND CEO OF JOANNA BLOOR

https://nanmckayconnects.com/2021/07/how-to-be-a-transformation-fairy-godmother-joanna-bloor/.

Joanna Bloor

Known for building teams, infrastructure, and revenue strategies through their moments of accelerating growth and rapid change, **Joanna Bloor** did so in environments where there were no rule books, no career paths, no precedents of how things "should" be done.

> *I heard a beautiful phrase the other day where somebody said that they were results-oriented but life-supporting, and I really like that idea. When I think about the path that I'm on, and the journey that I'm on, while I'm always keeping an ear to the ground to the traditional path, I am also giving myself permission to keep it a lifestyle business. I'm waiting to see where both the business and my customers lead me because they inevitably are my guideposts.*

* * *

For a lifestyle entrepreneur, the lifestyle becomes the feature, and the career is built around the lifestyle. The business will usually make money because that is necessary for most of us to have any positive lifestyle at all. The difference is that the money supports the lifestyle, which is the primary focus.

Sometimes you can achieve a lifestyle business by creating passive income. For example, an author publishes a book, which has ongoing sales. An online course is recorded. Webinars are recorded and accessed remotely. These are called evergreen products because, once built, they continue to provide revenue with very little additional work. Marketing will continue, but the additional effort is minor in comparison to the day-to-day work of running a traditional business. This passive income can drive your purpose and profits. This kind of evergreen business is currently one of the most popular business models.

For lifestyle entrepreneurs who are described as digital nomads, the emphasis is on freedom and is often associated with people who love to travel and don't want to be tied down to one location. Digital nomads prize working on their own schedule, setting their hours and time frame. If they are able to generate enough money to sustain their passion, they are content with fewer hours and less business growth.

Because data is stored in the cloud, we don't have to drag around a big mainframe. Traveling with a laptop, a smartphone, and a jetpack or hotspot to connect to the internet is usually sufficient to get the work done. If we need a printer, one is usually available not far away.

INSIGHTS ON LIFESTYLE ENTREPRENEURSHIP

INTERVIEW WITH **CASE LANE**,

FORMER DIPLOMAT IN THE CANADIAN FOREIGN SERVICE AND AUTHOR OF NINETEEN BOOKS, INCLUDING *RECAST: THE ASPIRING ENTREPRENEUR'S PRACTICAL GUIDE TO GETTING STARTED WITH AN ONLINE BUSINESS*

https://nanmckayconnects.com/2020/08/case-lane-2/

Case Lane

Case Lane is an entrepreneur, global writer, traveler, and observer to the future. She helps people achieve lifestyle freedom by fulfilling their dream to become an entrepreneur through her website, Ready Entrepreneur, podcasts, books, and courses. Having experienced both, she describes the difference between lifestyle and traditional entrepreneurship.

One of the challenges when you work in corporate or anywhere is taking time off. I have friends all over the world, and they live in countries that I would visit. You want to be able to just go and enjoy yourself and not feel that you are cutting your vacation short to rush back home trying to cover for the office. It was a big thing for me to realize what online business was all about. And how you're not only doing work you really want to do, but you're also doing it on your terms.

That doesn't mean that you get to just put your feet up. If nothing happens, you might end up working a lot more. The difference is that you control it. You organize it closer to around the schedule of the other things you want to do. You don't end up in that situation that you have quite often in corporate life, where you're having to give up something like your sister's getting married, and you go just for the wedding on Saturday, but you'd rather have gone for a week to help out and get things organized.

Or you have that vacation that you want to take, and you'd really love to explore a country for a month, but you can only go for a week. Or even just how you like to work. You have to be at the office at 9 a.m., but you're really a late-night person. You do your best work at midnight. You'd like to be able to organize your life around the way that you really like to work.

I think it is a surprise for people to realize you can do that. So many of us grow up with the traditional path to go to college and get a good job and then save for retirement and retire. That's the end of it. Because we're living the instruction we've been given a long time ago, we think that that's the only thing we can do. And that's what we see most people doing.

But when you start to get into lifestyle business such as an online business, you realize that there are all these people right now earning a living strictly online and living their life on their own terms. And when you start to realize that that's an option for you, that starts to look pretty good. Even if the work is going to take you months or years to get to the point where you could do that, when that's the outcome, and you can then live your life like that for as long as you like, you know that it's worth it to put in the time upfront.

* * *

Lifestyle entrepreneurship isn't for everyone. Not everyone has the freedom because kids are in school, or you are saving for college expenses. Maybe you are caring for an elderly or ill spouse or parent? It may be easier if you are single rather than responsible for a family.

Maybe you have financial commitments. But maybe you can set your lifestyle financial standard and design the business to meet it. Maybe you can prepare for it, even if you can't do it right now. But maybe it's something to think about, depending on your financial parameters, your skills, your home life, and your interests.

You will have highs and lows, but you have had these in your job as well. If you have more highs than lows, the change will be worth it. If you are looking for freedom and working on something that really interests you and are willing to put in the work, regardless of the time and energy the launch and operation takes, entrepreneurship may be exactly what you are looking for. Walk into the business endeavor with your eyes wide open. Walk toward it because you want to have the business, not because you are running away from something else. If the little spark inside you says, "I want this!" then go grab it. We will hold your hand along the path to avoid the tripping hazards to grow that spark into a flame that burns inside you.

ACTION STEP 4.

LIFESTYLE ENTREPRENEUR OR TRADITIONAL ENTREPRENEUR?

What lifestyle are you looking for?

- ☐ Spend more time with your friends and family
- ☐ Make your work schedule fit your own schedule
- ☐ Focus on the skills you already have, rather than honing new skills
- ☐ Create substantial personal growth potential
- ☐ Obtain the freedom and flexibility to follow your passion and still make money
- ☐ If you checked most of these, you are more of a lifestyle entrepreneur

A business can take many forms, as you will see when we list many business ideas for you to consider. Identifying why you want to make the change and start a business will help you when you are trying to clarify what business to choose. Start by analyzing your reasons for starting a business. What is your motivation? Which reason excites you the most?

Where do you find your right expertise? You may have an expertise, but that area may not interest you anymore or you may be tired of it.

INSIGHTS ON STAYING WITH YOUR EXPERTISE

NAN MCKAY, FOUNDER

AND PRESIDENT OF NAN MCKAY AND ASSOCIATES

https://nanmckayconnects.com/about

Nan McKay

When I left a government career I felt I had mastered and decided to start a business, I had expertise in operating and managing a specific government housing program. But I also had been fascinated by manage- ment and supervision. I had spoken at many confer- ences and written several books on both the housing program operation and supervisory management.

My idea was to totally leave the housing field with the "been there, done that" attitude and become a supervisory management trainer. As I was exploring this idea, I read several books like *What Color Is Your Parachute?* (Ten Speed Press) and *The Inventurers: Excursions in Life and Career Renewal* (Perseus Publishing). I met with the author, Jan Hagberg, of *The Inventurers*, a book that is still available through Amazon today. Jan gave me some very good advice. She said, "Your expertise is in the subsidized housing field. Don't run away from your expertise area. Just do something different in that area using other skills." And that was the beginning of a small company started out of the basement of my house that has grown into a large successful company today.

* * *

INTERVIEW WITH **DEBRA WOOG**, FOUNDER AND CEO OF CONNECT2 CORPORATION

https://nanmckayconnects.com/2021/09/how-to-help-navigate-crisis-debra-woog/

Debra Woog

Debra Woog is a crisis navigation partner who provides leaders with expertise, structure, and empathy. Woog helps people process difficult situations, connect with necessary resources, communicate effectively, and lead with a clear mind and solid strategy. In her interview, she explains how she would help a woman choose a business and references using a SWOT analysis.

Two years ago, I decided to refocus on the theme of crisis, realizing that I had been helping people in crises since I was a teenager. I was always one of those people who went to difficult situations. I've been doing this my whole life without knowing it had a name. It has been an amazing experience to feel like I have been doing exactly what I meant to be doing.

* * *

ACTION STEP 5.

MY MOTIVATIONS AND BENEFITS

What is your motivation for starting a business? Start with the *why*. Why do you want to start a business? Which reason excites you the most?

- ☐ I want to work from home.
- ☐ I want to have freedom and flexibility.
- ☐ I want to have extra income.
- ☐ I want to share my creative passion.
- ☐ I want to be independent.
- ☐ I have a mission to fulfill.
- ☐ I see a niche opportunity.

CHAPTER 3 TAKEAWAYS

VISUALIZE A BUSINESS DRIVING YOUR PASSION, PURPOSE, AND PROFIT

- Embracing lifestyle and problem-solving entrepreneurship.
- Pivoting to lifestyle and social entrepreneurship, plus components of lifestyle entrepreneurship.
- Creating a product as a social entrepreneur—understanding the purpose of a lifestyle entrepreneur.
- Traditional entrepreneur versus lifestyle entrepreneur.
- Are you prepared to become a lifestyle entrepreneur?
- Stay with your expertise and assess your strengths—don't run away from your expertise; look for something different in that area.
- Finding your reason for starting a business.

CHAPTER 4

EXPLORE AND CHOOSE YOUR BUSINESS

If you want to start a business, look at which sectors are growing the fastest. First, you have options and, second, you may want to consider the faster-growing sector as you choose the kind of business you would like to create. The opportunity area of entrepreneurship continues to grow. In the 2019 State of Women-Owned Businesses Report,[10] women-owned businesses grew 21 percent between 2014 and 2019, compared to 9 percent in overall business growth. Businesses owned by women of color grew by 43 percent!

You have thought about why you want to start a business, whether you want your company to be a lifestyle business, and what needs your business will serve. Now you want to select the right business for *you*. If you are going to put the time and effort needed into starting a business, do some research and some thinking. You want to find a business that fits your education, time, and money, but if you want to be a lifestyle entrepreneur, the business must also fit you—your mission, your passion, or your opportunity.

INSIGHTS INTO CHOOSING A BUSINESS

INTERVIEW WITH **DEBRA WOOG**,

FOUNDER AND CEO OF CONNECT2 CORPORATION

https://nanmckayconnects.com/2021/09/how-to-help-navigate-crisis-debra-woog/

Debra Woog

I would want to understand what she has in mind as the vision for starting the business. I would want to understand what she's looking for and why she is choosing to start the business. What is the business about? What does she think that her strategic advantages are?

10. https://s1.q4cdn.com/692158879/files/doc_library/file/2019-state-of-women-owned-businesses-report.pdf

I would do a SWOT analysis to determine the strengths and the weaknesses and the opportunities and the threats. She should go into it with eyes wide open. At the same time, do not wait till everything in your life and your career feels like it is perfectly aligned before starting. I can tell you from my own experience and watching all of my clients and my own professional network, there is no perfect time to start. And very rarely do people feel fully ready. And that is okay. Being an entrepreneur means being a lifelong learner and getting used to not knowing everything and learning some things on the fly.

* * *

One of the primary questions is income-related. Do you need to replace the income you currently have? Or is the income a secondary factor, which means profit is not your primary motive? Simply put, the profit motive suggests that people tend to take actions that will result in them making money. Profit is the basic motivation for any business, but the profit motivation must be tempered with humanity, respect, and ethics to be successful for the long term.

INSIGHTS ON HOW MUCH MONEY YOU NEED

INTERVIEW WITH **DEBRA WOOG**,

FOUNDER AND CEO OF CONNECT2 CORPORATION

https://nanmckayconnects.com/2021/09/how-to-help-navigate-crisis-debra-woog/

Debra Woog

I am a single parent. I am not living off somebody else's income or trust fund. I borrowed some money from the equity in my house to make that pivot. But I feel like there was no better bet than investing in myself. And that investment has paid off. Get creative looking for support. See what you can do without. Can you lower your expenses in some areas while you're building up? You don't have to earn your corporate salary if you start your own business, because you won't have some of the corporate expenses anymore. If you start your own business, and you are working from home, you won't need to wear pantyhose every day. How many pairs of pantyhose did we all have to buy when having to dress up to go work in a corporate environment? Dry cleaning bills—you won't have those. Instead of assuming that you have to earn the equivalent of the gross of your former salary, really think about what the expenses are and how you might be able to go down in your amount of income initially without affecting your quality of life.

* * *

ACTION STEP 6.

ANALYZE YOUR NEEDS

What do you need out of the business? Check all that apply.

- ☐ Primary income
- ☐ Secondary income
- ☐ Something to be productive at
- ☐ Contribute to society
- ☐ Work remotely
- ☐ Work at something that pleases you
- ☐ Dedicate and teach
- ☐ Connect with friends and family
- ☐ Give back
- ☐ Be generous
- ☐ Keep the energy going
- ☐ Find new things to do
- ☐ Something else ______________________________

What kind of business will drive your passion, purpose, and profit? Do you want to sell products or services out of a store or online? As you weigh your options, you will feel like the options are endless.

Gold in the Golden Years provides insight into the development of today's primary business structure, an online lifestyle business. Consider what you could sell as related to your education and expertise. What do you know that others would want to buy? If you can integrate your knowledge and experience into an online environment, the startup costs are vastly different than a business with a physical storefront.

One of the fastest-growing sectors of business is the self-education industry. The demand for specialized programs, training, and coaching is an amazing opportunity area. In prior decades, women who wanted to change fields went back to school to get another degree. That educational endeavor required several years of effort. You either went to school while working, which I did and which takes much longer, or you quit work if you could afford to quit. Quitting work to go to school was a faster option, but you had to have the resources to be able to take this road.

We also had books such as the Dummies books and the self-help books. Often these books did not provide a blueprint or depth of understanding of the specific field. The books were helpful but were not an easy entry into another field.

Today, a new movement is present. People are looking for the practical skills needed to break into a field or pivot to another field. People are seeking knowledge from experienced people who have achieved results in their career or business. People are moving from the theoretical to the practical, part of the do-it-yourself (DIY) movement. The internet and YouTube have had a huge influence on this movement. The pandemic helped push this movement because people were stuck at home with only the internet for company.

Learners today are looking for a combination of resources and do not seem to mind if they are not in the same place with the same source. They wind their self-teaching together with short courses, webinars, books, boot camps, summits, and masterminds.

This new focus has two positives for women over fifty wanting to start a business. These women have years of experience and have gained extensive knowledge. Therefore, writing a book, conducting a webinar, or creating a course on a subject that people want to learn about will be consistent with your knowledge, skills, and abilities. A market is more likely for a variety of topics than ever before. The second positive is that you will need to acquire new skills, but education and information on those skills—usually related to online knowledge, skills, and abilities—are readily available on the internet. The startup costs for creating this kind of business are minimal in comparison to a business with a physical location.

Another new focus is coaching, which can also be done online. An experienced person, called a coach, supports a client or learner in achieving a specific personal or professional goal by providing training and guidance. Coaches are viewed as facilitators of learning. Instead of imparting knowledge or knowing the "right answer," coaches help their clients unlock their own potential. The client is the focus, and the key skill of a coach is to ask the right questions to help the individual work through issues, solve problems, and improve performance. The premise is that individuals have the answers to their own problems within themselves. Coaches focus on the *how*, not the *what* and the *why*. The objective is to improve skills and raise the competence level of clients.

An excellent guide to finding your interests, hobbies, and passions can be found here: https://www.iloveit.net/list/list-of-passions-hobbies-and-interests/.

ACTION STEP 7.

PASSIONS, HOBBIES, AND INTERESTS

The guide above lists these broad categories and allows you to click on the broad categories for many passions, hobbies, and interests within each category. Check off the category or categories you are most interested in.

- ☐ Hobbies and Activities
- ☐ Culture and Entertainment
- ☐ Personal Development
- ☐ Business
- ☐ Food and Drink
- ☐ Lifestyle
- ☐ Family and Relationships
- ☐ Nature and Outdoors
- ☐ Sports
- ☐ Technology

What is the best business for you? What do you need out of the business? Does your business choice match your strengths? What are the knowledge, skills, and abilities you will need for this business? Let's find the right business, the right launch, the right customer, and the right combination for success for *you*.

ACTION STEP 8.

POTENTIAL BUSINESS IDEAS

What type of business appeals to you? Check off the businesses that hold a strong interest for you and you feel you have the knowledge, skills, and ability to start a business in this area.

Physical Products

- ☐ Clothing line (online; e.g., T-shirts)
- ☐ Fashion store online
- ☐ Flea market flipper (sell on eBay)
- ☐ Homemade/company products to sell online
- ☐ Pet products
- ☐ Print-on-demand—customize product with your design (books, hats, backpacks, blankets, pillows, mugs, shoes, hoodies, phone cases, watches)
- ☐ T-shirts
- ☐ Reseller—buy in bulk and resell
- ☐ Sell print-on-demand shirts

Digital Products

- ☐ Affiliate marketing
- ☐ Amazon reseller
- ☐ Art (online)
- ☐ Author—write and publish a book (also could be listed under Physical Products)
- ☐ Blogger
- ☐ Digital offerings (courses, templates, music, licenses for digital assets like photos, membership sites, digital templates, and tools)
- ☐ Digital services
- ☐ Drop-shipping

- ☐ Handmade products
- ☐ Media (podcast, YouTube)
- ☐ Online course
- ☐ Print on demand
- ☐ Songwriting
- ☐ Virtual assistance—Upwork, Fiverr (someone who can take on the daily tasks and processes that are important for running your business)
- ☐ Web design

Service-Based

- ☐ Accounting or bookkeeping or tax advice
- ☐ Brewing or wine making
- ☐ Childcare
- ☐ Coach (business, lifestyle)
- ☐ Consultant (content marketing, search engine marketing)
- ☐ Fitness trainer
- ☐ Food service
- ☐ Freelancing—virtual assistant, Pinterest, copyediting, customer service (Upwork, Fiverr, Dribble, 99Designs)
- ☐ Freelance writing
- ☐ Gardening
- ☐ Home decorating
- ☐ Housecleaning
- ☐ House sitting
- ☐ In-home health care
- ☐ Landscaping
- ☐ Languages—teach, transcribe
- ☐ Life/business coach
- ☐ Notary loan signing agent
- ☐ Personal training
- ☐ Pet sitter, pet groomer, pet walker

- ☐ Digital photography
- ☐ Proofreader
- ☐ Real estate investing
- ☐ Sales
- ☐ Self-publishing
- ☐ Sell freelance services
- ☐ Sell digital products
- ☐ Soap making
- ☐ Social media marketing
- ☐ Social media manager
- ☐ Software coding
- ☐ Stock trader
- ☐ Transcriber
- ☐ Translator
- ☐ Travel agent
- ☐ Tutor
- ☐ Uber
- ☐ UX Designer
- ☐ Vegetable growing
- ☐ Website creator or maintenance

For a more complete list, go to https://www.nanmckayconnects.com/GoldPowerBonus and download the free list of potential businesses, with links to websites.

If you want to start your own business, but don't know where to start, follow these steps:

1. Start by thinking about your true passion—what do you want to do every day?

2. Think about a killer business idea and test the idea with the market. Make sure the business has a demand for it. Test who your target customer would be. Get to know them. Learn about them as much as you can.

3. Consider the skill set that you have and what you lack. When starting your own business, be the boss in the area that you're good at and hire someone to help you in the area that you're weak in. If you can't do that at first, sites to help you are available such as Upwork, Fiverr, and even Acadium with interns. And learn enough about the tasks to know whether you are getting quality work.

4. Take a leap of faith in yourself and start. If not now, when? You can't get your time back. You don't want to be too old and have regrets. Follow your dream. Don't waste any more time. Whether you succeed or fail, you will have learned a lot.

You have considerable information about the direction you might want to head. Now we will narrow the direction down into potential businesses.

ACTION STEP 9.

SELECT POTENTIAL BUSINESSES AND PRIORITIZE

Using any or all of the methods above, review your items with checked boxes in this Action Step. Now that you have more information, decide on the top five business ideas for you. Enter them with a priority number in the box.

BEST POTENTIAL BUSINESSES	PRIORITY
1.	
2.	
3.	
4.	
5.	

As we go through the steps, you may find that the business you have chosen is not the right business for you. That's fine. You have listed five possibilities. You may find that you combine or pare down your potential businesses. The thought process is what counts at this stage. If you are laboring over which business to choose, don't put yourself under undue pressure.

Remember that you are not usually making a decision that will be cut in stone, and you can usually change the plan. What you don't want to do is jump in without a plan and find that the decision you made was totally wrong for you, resulting in serious consequences in time or money. At that point, your only option is to return to your former job. And that may not realistically be an option. Or you may find you really miss your old job. You may or may not have the option to return, but nothing is wrong with taking that step if you have discovered you miss your old job too much.

INSIGHTS INTO MATCHING SKILLS WITH BUSINESS CHOICE

To help you choose a business, a self-assessment of your strengths and weaknesses as they relate to the business you are considering is very helpful. If you are weak in an area needed by our business choice, you can assess what it will take to acquire the knowledge, skills, or abilities needed to perform the business or, more importantly, whether you can hire or contract with someone else to cover your weakness areas. You may find that the more expedient and wise choice is to capitalize on the tasks you do well and hire someone else to do the tasks you are not proficient in, rather than try to learn everything and do everything yourself. Remember that "hiring someone" may simply be finding the right virtual assistant to help you.

INTERVIEW WITH **THRESETTE BRIGGS**, FOUNDER AND CEO OF PERFORMANCE 3

https://nanmckayconnects.com/2020/06/thresette-briggs/

Thresette Briggs

For the first step of your S.O.A.R. Launch and Growth Plan, it is critical to establish a strong mindset for long-term success on the journey, and to acknowledge that as a new business owner it may not be as easy to do this on your own. The skills it takes to succeed as your own boss are vastly different than what's needed to work for someone else, and three of the most important are leadership, accountability, and follow-through.

* * *

The purpose of a business is to solve a problem, a pain point, and get paid to do it. You already have skills to help people solve problems. You have been demonstrating your skills daily in your 9 to 5 job. Rather than finding a new business, why not use one of your existing skills? If you have been in company management, you have utilized many leadership skills. What skills are your top skills? Giving presentations? Establishing goals and objectives? Planning job assignments? Problem-solving?

ACTION STEP 10.

COMPLETE YOUR CURRENT LEADERSHIP SKILLS CHECKLIST

Assess your leadership skills, from 1 to 4, using the criteria below. The chart has three columns:

- **Need to Know**—something you don't yet know but feel you should. Use the rating scale on the chart to indicate your answer. Note that a 0 on the scale indicates "Not applicable to business." Only enter a 0 if you feel you do not have a need to develop your knowledge, skills, and abilities in this area.
- **Know Now**—a topic you do know. Indicate your level of knowledge of the topic using the rating scale for this column.
- **Needs Work**—if you either need to know it or it needs work, put a check mark in the box in this column.

So, you have a chart with four columns: (1) Skill, (2) Need to Know, (3) Know Now, and (4) Needs Work.

NEED TO KNOW	KNOW NOW	NEEDS WORK
Mark how important knowledge of the subject area is for your business	Mark how well you know the subject area	Check if you need to work on this subject area

4 = Crucial 3 = Extremely important 2 = Moderately important 1 = Not very important 0 = Not applicable	4 = Crucial 3 = Extremely important 2 = Moderately important 1 = Not very important 0 = Not applicable	

SUBJECT	NEED TO KNOW	KNOW NOW	NEEDS WORK
Computer software, hardware, and multi-user network systems			
Principles of public relations			
Advertising for a job opening in the department			
Hiring			
Interviewing prospective staff			
Utilizing staff resources and providing professional development opportunities			
Monitoring and measuring staff performance			
Completing a written performance evaluation			
Conducting staff performance evaluations			
Documenting performance problems			
Firing			
Establishing department goals and objectives			
Monitoring and measuring program performance			
Working with staff in establishing individual goals and objectives			
Planning job assignments			
Encouraging teamwork and fostering cooperation among staff			
Supervisor/board of directors/clients			
Roles and responsibilities of CEO, board, and program staff			
Mediating staff issues and conflicts			

Problem-solving			
How to service irate customers			
How to coordinate supportive services			
How to develop and launch a successful marketing plan and conduct program outreach			
Clear spoken and written communication skills			
Active listening skills			
Research skills			
Analytical skills			
Reading comprehension skills			
Math skills			
Interpersonal skills for relating to a broad range of people			
Time management skills			
Public speaking skills			
Creative problem-solving skills			
Decision-making skills			
Budgeting skills			
Crisis management skills			
Training skills			
Business plan development			
Fostering positive culture			
Financial report analysis			
Social media and software apps			
Interviewing skills			
Leading and directing staff			
Identifying and implementing effective organizational structures			

Were you amazed at the skills you currently have? With these skills, you could sell a service such as consulting, coaching, or freelancing. Could you write a blog, or even a book, on any of these areas? Your badass killer idea is probably germinating right now. Many people are writing a book because Amazon has made self-publishing an easy reality for most people. And you can even get paid for your blogging! You know more than you think you know! You just need to unlock it.

ACTION STEP 11.

ASSESS KNOWLEDGE, SKILLS, AND ABILITIES (KSAs) NEEDED FOR YOUR BUSINESS CHOICE VERSUS YOUR CURRENT SKILLS

All businesses have knowledge, skills, and abilities (KSA) requirements. To accurately assess strengths and weaknesses, you need to evaluate your current KSAs against the KSAs that are required to perform the required duties of the business. Analyze some or all of your business choices to determine what KSAs that business needs. You can then assess what KSAs you have versus what KSAs you will need. You may need to take classes or develop skills to conduct the business. If you find the stretch is too big to obtain the KSAs in the time frame you need, you can move on to another business choice.

Knowledge, what you know or understand, is information that makes the performance of the job possible.

Skills are what you have learned to do. They are readily observable, quantifiable, or measurable.

Ability is the capacity to perform an activity.

The chart helps to identify:

- What you need to know or be able to do
- How familiar you are with a specific subject area
- Whether more work is needed on the topic

Starting with your first priority, think about the knowledge, skills, and abilities that will be needed to conduct a business you would be interested in. Enter those in the chart below.

Then assess your knowledge, skills, and abilities by using the criteria below to evaluate. The chart has three columns (as also shown in Action Step 10 above).

NEED TO KNOW	KNOW NOW	NEEDS WORK
Mark how important knowledge of the subject area is for your business	Mark how well you know the subject area	Check if you need to work on this subject area
4 = Crucial 3 = Extremely important 2 = Moderately important 1 = Not very important 0 = Not applicable	4 = Expert 3 = High knowledge 2 = Moderate knowledge 1 = Little knowledge 0 = No knowledge at all	

SUBJECT	NEED TO KNOW	KNOW NOW	NEEDS WORK
KSAs for My Business Choice			

SUBJECT	NEED TO KNOW	KNOW NOW	NEEDS WORK

If you feel your KSAs are not a good match with the business, select your next highest priority and do the chart again.

NEED TO KNOW	KNOW NOW	NEEDS WORK
Mark how important knowledge of the subject area is for your business	Mark how well you know the subject area	Check if you need to work on this subject area
4 = Crucial 3 = Extremely important 2 = Moderately important 1 = Not very important 0 = Not applicable	4 = Expert 3 = High knowledge 2 = Moderate knowledge 1 = Little knowledge 0 = No knowledge at all	

SUBJECT	NEED TO KNOW	KNOW NOW	NEEDS WORK
KSAs for My Business Choice			

Everyone has a strength he or she can bring to the table. You may not feel like the ultimate expert, but people aren't looking for that. They simply want someone who knows more than they do and can explain that area so that it's easy to understand. The more people buy into your expertise, the more expertise you are thought to have.

Who are you? Who are you meant to be? What interests you? What gets you excited about doing it? We need to step back and think about our personality or behavior style, aptitude, interests, and values. These areas of interest will help you decide what you need in a job to make the job fulfilling to you. Although many things have changed over your life, what hasn't changed is your personality type and your temperament. Thinking about these areas in relation to a job are the keys to finding a more fulfilling second career.

Three assessments will help you find out more about yourself to choose the right business:

- **Assessment on Oprah's site:** Who Am I Meant to Be?
- **ASK Method Assessment:** Choose Your Business
- **DiSC Profile**

ASSESSMENT ON OPRAH'S SITE

An assessment that is quick to take and free can be found here: https://www.oprah.com/inspiration/who-are-you-meant-to-be-self-assessment-quiz_1.

Anne Dranitsaris, PhD, who developed the quiz, describes the model as "This quiz can help you figure out what really defines you. Based on personality science, I have identified seven 'striving styles,' modes of thought and behavior that direct us to seek satisfaction in different ways. Although everybody is wired with all seven styles, most people have one that dominates. When you engage this innate style, you've got the best shot at fulfilling your potential; when you don't, you can feel stuck."

ASK METHOD ASSESSMENT

The ASK Method Company is a three-time *Inc.* 5000 company and was most recently named the seventh fastest growing company in Austin, Texas, and the fiftieth fastest growing educational company in the United States.

Ryan Levesque provides training in a variety of areas. The ASK Method website has an assessment that will be especially valuable if you are considering an online business. There are nearly thirty different types of online marketing funnels. Take this quiz to find out which one is right for you and your business. Levesque's assessment will let you discover your entrepreneur type, which product you should sell based on your personality, and what type of business model you should go into based on your resources, your goals, and the lifestyle you want.

This free ASK Method Assessment can be found on his site: https://choosequiz.com/quiz-6-2/

Every assessment you take to find the business best suited to you will provide insight to help in your exploration. You can then analyze the data to discover the business model best matched to you.

DISC PROFILE ASSESSMENT

The DiSC profile is one of the assessments that is very helpful in discovering your behavioral style/personality type. In working with the DiSC profile since the early 1990s and after teaching the basics of this model in many executive management classes, I have found the model to be as accurate as you were in completing the questions. The DiSC profile describes four styles: Dominance, Influence, Steadiness, and Cautious/Compliant. Each style has recognizable behaviors as well as strengths and vulnerabilities. Behavior styles are not good or bad.

A strong Dominance style means shaping the environment by overcoming opposition to accomplish results. High Ds are task-oriented. A High I influencer style places the emphasis on shaping the environment by influencing or persuading others. High Is are people-oriented. A High S steadiness style the emphasis on cooperating and sharing responsibilities with others within existing circumstances to carry out the tasks. High Ss like a predictable environment and do not prefer change. A high C cautious, conscientious style enjoys working within existing circumstances to ensure quality and accuracy. And, of course, combinations of the styles are normal.

The reason understanding these styles is important is to further your understanding of yourself and those around you. And when you are seeking a career you enjoy, the styles can play a direct role. For example, if you are a high I and like people, a job that involves data entry all day would probably cause you to interrupt yourself many times just to communicate with others. If you have a high D style, you prefer being in charge or at least having strong input into how the job was done. If you have a high S style, a job where the priorities change quickly and often would not be satisfying to you. And if you have a high C style, taking a job where you are rushed and where quality and accuracy don't matter would frustrate you. Depending on how strong the style is for you, the higher level of job satisfaction or frustration would affect your performance in the job, especially over a long period of time.

For a full assessment, you can purchase a behavioral style questionnaire here: https://www.discprofile.com/what-is-disc.

I find if I answer these assessments as honest and true as I can—focusing on what is, not what I want the answer to be—they are usually right on.

The answers to the assessments will probably tie into how you like to work. Do you want to work alone, by project, for others, or with others?

All of these questions are important because you want to choose a business that will make you happy—a business that makes you want to jump out of bed (or stay up late depending on your energy cycle). If you understand who you are and how you like to work, if you decide on and follow your true passion, and if you think about what makes you happiest, you will enjoy almost every day of work. You will find the joy you are seeking. As you see in the following chapters, finding the joy won't necessarily be easy. Much work is to be done. But if you love what you do, the work won't seem like work.

Resource: A book that will help you match your work to your personality type is *Do What You Are* by Paul D. Tieger, Barbara Barron, and Kelly Tieger. One of their points in their book is that "The secret of career satisfaction lies in doing what you enjoy most."

ACTION STEP 12.

MATCH YOUR STRENGTHS TO BUSINESS CHOICES

What could I sell in relation to my education and expertise?

____

____

What do I know and understand that others would want to buy?

____

____

Is an online business a feasible option for me?

____

____

On the assessment on Oprah's site, what are my strengths?

___

___

On the ASK Method assessment, what entrepreneur type am I, which product should I sell, and what business model should I go into?

___

___

On the DiSC profile, which point or points are above the middle line on the graph? In reading over the strengths, are these correct?

___

___

In reviewing the assessment responses, what are my primary strengths?

___

___

How will my primary strengths match to the business needs?

___

___

INSIGHTS ON CHOOSING AND STARTING A BUSINESS

INTERVIEW WITH **ROBIN SHAPIRO**,

FOUNDER AND CEO OF HEALTH PERSPECTIVES GROUP AND AUTHOR OF *THE SECRET LANGUAGE OF HEALTH CARE*

https://nanmckayconnects.com/2021/09/how-to-advocate-for-the-healthcare-you-deserve-robin-shapiro/

Robin Shapiro

Robin Shapiro is the founder of many for-profit and nonprofit organizations, all having to do with health advocacy. Robin is currently Board Chair of HealthAdvocateX, a national nonprofit dedicated to helping people transform from patients to active participants and partners in their own care. She's also a published author of *The Secret Language of Healthcare: How to Ask for the Care You Deserve.*

What do I want to do with my life? I had a little bit of severance. I had two young babies at home. I hired a friend of mine to help me think it through. If I were to start a business, what would it be? I loved working with patients. I founded Health Advocacy Strategies in 2002. What I would say to people who might be on the edge of thinking about starting something is, "Do it. Do it. What do you have to lose?" It's a risk, and a lot of people are fearful. Challenge abounds in starting a business, but you will have fun in its creativity. If you are a creative can-do person, being your own boss is fantastic. Creating things. It's a divine experience. I'm a very spiritual person. And I feel like being an entrepreneur is a little bit divine.

* * *

The point is that you are in control of your life. The business decision is not just a one-shot alternative. You may discover a new or fresh challenge along the way that you would not have thought of in the beginning. Nothing says you can't pivot again. If you give yourself the gift of planning, gathering the facts before you leap, you stand a much better chance that the water isn't too deep and, in fact, is just right.

ACTION STEP 13.

SUMMARIZE YOUR ANALYSIS AND CHOOSE YOUR BUSINESS

The business idea I choose is:

____

____

After the analysis you have completed in the preceding chapters, this action step is the place to summarize your conclusions. The answers are purely for you. You now can pull everything you have learned together and put your conclusions in one place.

Who am I?

____

____

Why do I want to start a business?

____

____

What do I want from my business? Am I more of a lifestyle entrepreneur or a traditional entrepreneur?

How do my strengths match my business? What are the primary strengths needed for my business? What are my primary strengths?

When will I be ready to dive into entrepreneurship? Should I do a side hustle first?

Do my interests line up with my current expertise? What credentials do I need before I start?

What is my number 1 business choice, based on all of the above? What is my number 2 choice? What is my number 3 choice?

Do my KSAs match with my business choice? Where are the gaps? How will I fill these gaps?

____

____

List your business choice that matches your experience and expertise. In the third column, rate the competitive advantage you think you have in this business area from 1 to 5, with 5 being the highest. In column four, state why you gave the Competitive Advantage rating you did.

BEST BUSINESS CHOICE	PRIORITY	COMPETITIVE ADVANTAGE	WHY?

What facts do you have about the competitive advantage for each area?

____

____

What effect will the competitive advantage have on your decision?

____

____

What is the best choice for your business?

____

____

When you have made your decision, write a short description of what your business will do. Think of the description as turning your good idea into a viable business.

Then, shortly and succinctly, tell a friend what business you are going to start. The friend may ask you questions, helping you to further define the outcomes of your business. You may be too broad in your description, but the description will help you narrow your business idea down. The more specific you can be, the better. Go to Google and put your idea in. Look at the results to help you further define the business. Start with "I want to . . ." and narrow your idea down further until you synthesize your idea and can easily explain your business concept to others.

ACTION STEP 14.

TEST YOUR BUSINESS CHOICE

Now that you have decided in which direction you want to head, test your business choice. You might be interested in an area, but it's also important to look at key business drivers to determine whether a match is present. Business drivers are the key inputs and activities that drive the operational and financial results of a business. Common examples of business drivers are salespeople, number of stores, website traffic, number and price of products sold, and units of production. Even if you plan to start a small, online business, each business has market qualifiers. Let's explore some questions to get started:

1. Is a business need present? You need people to buy your product or service, and you should focus on their pain point to determine whether they will need your product. Is the business a solution or just something nice to have? How will you know?
2. Is this a knowledgeable area for you, and do you have the management and execution skills to carry this business idea out? Do

you have a background in this area? What will you need to learn? Can someone else help you?

3. Are you considering being a social entrepreneur? Nonprofits are usually engaged in fund-raising. How do you feel about doing that task?
4. How are you going to fund the business initially? Are you going to fund the business yourself or through friends and family?
5. How are you going to get noticed above the competition? Marketing in any area is required. Are you going to have to learn how to use social media?

One of the best tests to perform is a SWOT analysis, which analyzes your Strengths, Weaknesses, Opportunities, and Threats. SWOT analysis is a strategic planning technique used to help a person or organization identify strengths, weaknesses, opportunities, and threats related to business competition or project planning. A good reference with a template can be found at https://www.liveplan.com/blog/what-is-a-swot-analysis-and-how-to-do-it-right-with-examples/.

CHAPTER 4 TAKEAWAYS

EXPLORE AND CHOOSE YOUR BUSINESS

- How to choose a business that fits you—the important questions to ask.
- How much money you need—planning ahead on what's needed.

ANALYZE YOUR NEEDS

- Examples of businesses to start—self-education and coaching
- Online business—research on an interesting and fulfilling online business

ASSESSING YOUR STRENGTHS

- Choose the right business according to your personality by taking assessment tests
- Review your current leadership skills
- Three assessment test types and their importance when choosing a business

PASSIONS, HOBBIES, AND INTERESTS

- Explore and check your hobbies, interests, and passions to find the right business for you

POTENTIAL BUSINESS IDEAS

- Start a business in an area in which you have knowledge, skills, ability, and interest
- Steps to help guide you if you want to start your own business but don't know where to start

SELECT POTENTIAL BUSINESSES AND PRIORITIZE

- Let your knowledge, skills, and abilities (KSAs) guide you in business idea prioritization
- Prioritize no more than five businesses

SUMMARIZE YOUR ANALYSIS AND CHOOSE YOUR BUSINESS

- Summarize your findings from your business analysis. List your first business choice

CHAPTER 5

SET YOUR GOALS

These steps will guide you through the goal-setting process:

STEP 1: DEFINE THE OBJECTIVE

What is the outcome to be achieved? Define the desired outcome. If you have others who will implement the goal, your objective can be set with the participation of those who are most knowledgeable and will be directly involved in the process. By defining objectives, you provide a way to measure the movement toward the vision. Strategy turns visions into reality and is the crossover mechanism between where you are now and the desired future. Objectives are stated in precise, measurable terms.

ACTION STEP 15.

WRITE MY OBJECTIVE IN THIS BUSINESS

Write a clear objective that you can return to and review your progress as you develop your business.

____

____

____

STEP 2: DEFINE AND WRITE THE GOAL USING THE SMART CRITERIA

Creating the goal also includes defining the action steps (tasks) that are needed to achieve the goal. Tasks are concrete, measurable events that must occur. Review all of the data you have gathered to date. You now should have some data to make some fact-based goals rather than emotional goals. Setting a goal is how we move from an idea to reality. A clear definition of a goal is *a written statement that clearly describes certain actions or tasks with a measurable end result.* A measurable goal is quantifiable and is described in such a way that the actual result cannot be disputed. If you cannot measure it, chances are you cannot effectively manage it.

Each goal should meet this test:

- **Specific**—clear, understandable language
- **Measurable**—quantifiable, amounts, numbers, percentages
- **Attainable**—perhaps difficult, but not impossible
- **Relevant**—supports next higher-level goals and mission
- **Time-bound**—includes a start time, progress milestones, and end dates

ACTION STEP 16.

SET YOUR GOALS

Use this format to set your goals and then check to see if they meet the goal test or criteria. Write five goals, starting with your number one priority.

GOAL #	DESCRIPTION	SPECIFIC	MEASURABLE	ATTAINABLE	RELEVANT	TIME-BOUND

STEP 3: DEVELOP AN ACTION PLAN

The final step is to follow up and validate that you and the team are doing what is required. You want to validate that the goals are worthy of the effort. For the leader, this step demonstrates the commitment to success in accomplishing the goal. Note that validation does not mean to micro-manage. Micro-management undermines the confidence of others; following up simply ensures that the desired activities are being done as planned.

ACTION STEP 17.

DEVELOP AN ACTION PLAN

Creating an action plan for each goal is important throughout your business life. An action plan will tell you who is going to do what, by when. This format makes creating an action plan much easier. If your goal is comprehensive and has many moving parts over a longer period of time, you can create a project plan. Software to do a project plan with milestones is available on the market.

GOAL #	TASK	PERSON RESPONSIBLE	START DATE	END DATE	EXTENSION DATE	APPROVAL

Now that you have a written goal, what steps can you take to ensure you achieve the goal?

- Regularly and vividly imagine your goal as accomplished.
- Share your goal with as many people as possible so they can support and encourage your actions to achieve the goal.

- Break the goal down into small steps or tasks and set deadlines to complete the smaller steps.
- Review your progress regularly.
- Plan each task or step on your calendar by making an appointment to work on a particular part of the task. Block out the time necessary and try not to allow interruptions, phone calls, or other tasks to distract you.
- If you are having trouble or getting backlogged, ask for help. Also, allow yourself time to help others who may be backlogged as well.
- Make the decision that you will accomplish the goal.
- Plan a reward for yourself for the accomplishment of the goal. Even if no one else (like your boss) will provide a reward, you can reward yourself with something that is meaningful to you. Your reward could be booking a massage, buying that book you have been thinking about, allowing yourself to sit for 30 minutes without any tasks, or anything you might find pleasurable. This reward will also help to motivate you to accomplish the goal.

CHAPTER 5 TAKEAWAYS

SET YOUR GOALS

- Assess your KSAs—plan and gather the facts before starting a business and give yourself space to pivot along the way.
- Define the objective—what is the desired outcome?
- Write a clear objective and review your progress as you develop the business.
- Define and write the goal using the SMART criteria (Specific, Measurable, Attainable, Relevant, and Time-bound).
- Develop an action plan—steps to ensure you achieve your written goal.

SECTION II

ORGANIZE YOUR LAUNCH TO BE SUCCESSFUL AND FILLED WITH JOY

CHAPTER 6

CREATE A LEGAL FRAMEWORK FOR BUSINESS OPERATION

To have a successful launch, whether it is a first-time launch or you are relaunching, making sure you are covering all your bases and enjoying the process, you must organize, plan the structure, and prepare the necessary documents to operate the business legally and with clear direction. This plan may sound rudimentary, but if you have had a career in a larger firm, you probably did not participate in the initial preparation of launching a business. Other people were responsible. When you are the one launching the business, you need to create an organizational environment. As a solo entrepreneur, if you have been with a company that provided support staff to do many of the tasks, you may find you have an additional expertise learning curve.

Once you have made your decision to launch, you will be tempted to bypass the planning step and jump right into the operation. But before you open your doors, even if the doors are virtual, you need to set up this structure to ensure that you get off on the right foot and launch from a solid structure with necessary protections and plans in place.

INSIGHTS ON TRANSITIONING FROM CORPORATE TO SOLO ENTREPRENEUR

INTERVIEW WITH **LAURA YAMANAKA**,

FOUNDER AND CEO OF TEAMCFO

https://nanmckayconnects.com/2020/07/laura-yamanaka/

Laura Yamanaka

Because my business partner and I came out of large corporations, we thought we knew how to start a business and run a business because we've been doing this all along. We did a lot of mergers and acquisitions, taking over small businesses and growing them. I knew things like how to make a killer business plan and write a great pitch deck and never really thought about the fact of how you need capital. If we needed capital, we would just call up Uncle Jack. Hey, the money was always there. If you had an IT problem, you called the IT department or legal or HR. When you're a small business, you are the banker, the IT person, the legal person, you are HR. That was kind of shocking to us. And I think the biggest shock was the fact that we had all the trappings of a business. But when it comes down to it, you need to have a product or service, and you need to be able to sell it. If you don't have those first two things, all those other things are expensive. We learned very quickly that a great business plan and pitch deck does not make a good business product. We were fortunate that we were fast learners.

* * *

Your legal framework consists of the legal entity and status of your business. You will decide on your domain name, where you open your business bank account and credit card, the type of legal entity, whether any licenses or certifications are required to operate as a business, and how you are going to protect your intellectual property. You may want to consult an attorney and an accountant to help with some of your decision-making. Your state's Secretary of State office or similar agency's website will have considerable information on setting up your legal business entity status. I had this site assist me when I had to end my business in AZ and create a new business in WA. They did everything for me, and it was extremely well done and timely! You can reach them here: https://nanmckayconnects.com/corpnet.

DOMAIN NAME

Choose a name for your business. When you come up with a name you like, conduct a Google search on the internet to see if anyone else is using that name. If other people are already using that name, you may encounter legal consequences if you use the same or very similar name. Before you make your final decision, check domain names available for websites. You may want the same name for the business and the website. After your search is complete, purchase and register the domain name from an online vendor like GoDaddy. You may find the domain name you want but that name plus .com may not be available. Then you must decide whether the name you have selected is critical enough to risk the mix-up of .com versus the ending that is available, such as name.org or name.net.

In addition, each state usually has a department where you can check to confirm the business name's availability. For example, in Arizona, you would check domain name availability through the Arizona Corporation Commission. My recommendation is to check a site like GoDaddy first, then check your state's department. You do not want to skip this step, because if you change the name on your website, which is possible, you will have to deal with internal redirects. If you have considerable site traffic, you do not want to have it redirect every time someone attempts to visit the site.

The next step is to secure the name with the state. There are usually several options to consider. For example: https://azcc.gov/corporations/ten-steps-to-starting-a-business-in-az.

BUSINESS ADDRESS

Your decision on whether to include a business address on your website and documents that will be displayed publicly largely depends on whether you have an online business. If you have an online business in your home, you may not want your address displayed on the internet. If you do not have a storefront and are using your home for the business, you should consider obtaining a P.O. box to use instead of displaying an address.

BUSINESS BANK ACCOUNT

After you have selected and verified a domain name, you should set up a business bank account. You may even have to take this step first, as some state departments will not accept your temporary business check that lacks a preprinted name and address on them. I use my actual address, not a P.O. box, on my checking account. Check with the state department to determine whether you can pay by credit card.

CREDIT CARD

You may want a credit card in the business name. With a sole proprietorship or even an LLC, my advice for a sole proprietorship or LLC is to wait until you determine if you need a credit card in the business name or whether you can use your personal credit card. If you are establishing a corporation or partnership, you may want to consider securing a credit card in the business's name after setting up your legal entity. When you have an online business, you pay for almost everything with a credit card or through PayPal or Stripe. You establish a PayPal or Stripe account in your business name after you have established your business as a legal entity. Then, I recommend placing all of your business charges on one credit card. This procedure makes it much easier when you are doing your monthly accounting.

LEGAL ENTITY

A business entity is an organization created by an individual or individuals to conduct business, engage in a trade, or partake in similar activities. There are various types of business entities—sole proprietorship, partnership, LLC, corporation, S corporation, B corporation, and nonprofit.

You should fully understand the differences in the legal structures before you make your decision. Other than a sole proprietorship, these legal entities are set up within a state. Therefore, two sources to research are the department of your state that handles this function and the Small Business Association. You can conduct research online so you are familiar with the variety of legal structures available to you. Online sources helpful in this regard include https://incfile.com, Wikipedia definitions, and https://legalzoom.com. Again, https://nanmckayconnects.com/corpnet is very helpful in explaining your options.

A **sole proprietor** is one individual who owns a company that is not incorporated or registered with the state as a limited liability company (LLC). Sole proprietors may or may not have employees. The business does not exist separately from the owner. The risks of business apply to the individual's personal assets, including those not used for the business. The sole proprietor reports the business income on his or her individual tax return.

A **limited liability company (LLC)** provides protection for personal assets but is not a corporation. Typically, if you are forming an LLC, you will submit Articles of Organization. You should check with your state on its requirements. The business assets are owned by the LLC, not the owner. The LLC also reports business income on the individual's tax return. The liabilities are the liability of the business and do not have any impact on the individual owner's personal assets. Although any net profit or loss is included on the owner's personal tax return, other taxes such as payroll, sales, or property tax on owned business properties should be researched. Otherwise, the status is much the same as the sole proprietorship.

A **C corporation**, often referred to as a C corp, is a type of business entity that is formed and regulated on a state level. If you are forming a corporation, you will submit Articles of Incorporation. Be sure you have allowed for processing time because your documentation must be examined and approved by the state. The C corp also has limited liability. Stock must be issued, and ownership is determined by who holds the stock. A C corp is a more formal entity with a board of directors and numerous rules and regulations it must follow.

An **S corporation**, also referred to as an S corp, is for small corporations with a maximum of 100 shareholders. Owners can only get common stock. S corps have a requirement for a board of directors and have similar requirements to a C corp for holding meetings and keeping records. Similar to the LLC, the net profit or loss generated by an S corporation will flow through to the personal income tax returns of the shareholders and owners and be subject to the additional taxes identified for the LLC.

A **Certified B Corporation** is a relatively new legal entity option. The B Corp Certification is a third-party certification administered by the nonprofit B Lab, based in part on a company's verified performance on the B Impact Assessment. The benefit corporation is a legal structure for a business, like an LLC or a corporation. Certified B Corporations are businesses that meet the highest standards of verified social and environmental performance, public transparency, and legal accountability to balance profit and purpose. B Corps are accelerating a global culture shift to redefine success in business and build a more inclusive and sustainable economy. B Corps use profits and growth as a means to a greater end defined as a positive impact for their employees, communities, and the environment. B Corps form a community of leaders and drive a global movement of people using business as a force for good.

INSIGHTS ON A B CORP

INTERVIEW WITH **PAULA MARSHALL**,

CEO OF BAMA COMPANIES

https://nanmckayconnects.com/2021/07/how-to-employ-strategic-leadership-paula-marshall-purse-power/

Paula Marshall

Paula Marshall runs her organization with the philosophy of honoring everyone and helping people be successful. Her company is an example of a B Corp and won a Malcolm Baldrige National Quality Award.

B Corp is short for Benefit Corp. The B Corp is an IRS certification that you can hold, which is basically how you organize your people. How do you pay them? How do you help them grow in the community? Do you hire people with different economic backgrounds? What is your process to help people emerge from poverty?

It is about doing good in the world. It is about programs that you put in place that help the community demonstrate that business does not have to be just a profit organization, always chewing up resources. Business can be a force for good, but we have to plan it. We have to measure it. We have to know we are doing it, and why we're doing it.

Oftentimes, these things are not easy to do, and they do cost money. They do take time. I think if you read the B Corp certification, and you go in and look at the tests, the criteria to become a B Corp, there is nothing in there that is not going to make you a better company. It is all going to make you better.

It is about where do you want to focus your time. Do you want to work on your internal structures? Do you want to work on a volunteerism program so that people can go out in the community and volunteer? Do you want to work on structuring, flattening your wages across the board? It is a different philosophy, a philosophy about being a force for good. That philosophy could be with your own team members. Or it could be with your community, or it could be with your investors or your banks. It is all about where I can do good. And where can I maximize the places that I can do good?

I always looked at it as having a dual bottom line. Finances are also a part of the goal of a B Corp because the goal is not to do so many things that you go out of business. The goal of a B Corp is that you grow, but you grow with kind of a sustainability. When I talk about sustainability, most people think I'm talking about the resources around us, like water, air, the energy, the systems that we use, and those types of things.

Instead, a B Corp is an umbrella, more about how we treat people, how we pay people, and sustainability is definitely a part of that. But it is all about being good for the planet and showing people that business can be a force for good. Absolutely. And a huge force for good.

* * *

The **nonprofit corporation** is a type of corporation that is allowed to create profits which are used to preserve and expand the nonprofit. Nonprofits do not have owners but do have boards of directors. You can start a nonprofit, but you cannot technically own the nonprofit. One of the biggest advantages is that you are granted access to public and private grants. Any revenues generated must achieve a specific goal that is of public benefit. Nonprofits are formed by filing articles of incorporation in the state in which the nonprofit will operate. Nonprofits provide personal asset protection, which shields you from being personally liable for business debts. The nonprofit is tax exempt if it has the 501(c)(3) status.

INSIGHTS ON NONPROFIT CORPORATIONS

WRITTEN BY **LYN BURTON**,

EXECUTIVE DIRECTOR, AFFORDABLE HOUSING CONNECTIONS, AHC EDUCATION AND LEADERSHIP CENTER, USING MATERIAL FROM THE MINNESOTA COUNCIL OF NONPROFITS, OF WHICH AHC IS A MEMBER.

https://nanmckayconnects.com/2020/12/lyn-burton-2/

Lyn Burton

If you are starting a nonprofit business, you will need to be grounded in principles of accountability that may be different than a for-profit business. Your legal counsel and accountant will be your most valuable advisors and will help you decide the best legal structure for the type of nonprofit you envision. You should pay special attention to your Articles of Incorporation and Bylaws. In addition to areas common to all business models—planning, evaluation, human resources, and financial management—here are some additional key areas to consider:

- Governance
- Accountability and transparency
- Public policy and civic engagement
- Fundraising
- Volunteer management

These are some broad descriptions of areas that you need to be aware of in setting up a nonprofit organization.

GOVERNANCE

- A nonprofit is governed by a volunteer board of directors that establishes the process for the organization's mission, provides overall leadership and strategic direction to the organization, and acts as stewards of the organization's mission and resources. Boards of directors are not the owners of the nonprofit organization. They act in a variety of legal and fiduciary roles. As volunteers, unlike directors of for-profit companies, they are not paid for their service on the board.
- The board supervises the executive director, has overall responsibility for the organization, should represent the constituencies served by the mission, and as volunteer community members ensure that the public interest is served by the organization. The board should develop written administration, management, and oversight policies and practices consistent with any federal or state-recommended rules and suggested best practices.

ACCOUNTABILITY AND TRANSPARENCY

- A nonprofit must comply with all legally required reporting procedures, including filing the IRS Form 990 and annual reports as required by its state statutes.
- Unlike many private businesses, a nonprofit organization must make public disclosure of its financial information, including income and expense statement, balance sheet, and functional expense allocation, as well as a list of board members, management, staff, and contributors.

PUBLIC POLICY AND CIVIC ENGAGEMENT

- Nonprofit organizations are able to promote participation in public policymaking that furthers their mission, including advocacy, voter awareness, and even lobbying on issues and policies that impact their mission (subject to disclosure and reporting transparency).
- Nonprofits organized under IRS 501(c)(3) are prohibited from advocating partisan positions and fundraising or campaigning for partisan candidates.

FUNDRAISING

- Fundraising rules are complex since many donors prefer to keep their identity confidential, while IRS rules require transparency and disclosure.
- You must document receipt of donor funds in writing; donor intent related to restrictions must be honored, wherever possible; and funds must be subject to ethical standards of stewardship in the public interest, in keeping with your nonprofit organization's mission.
- The nonprofit organization must comply with all federal and state financial management and accounting and audit requirements.

VOLUNTEER MANAGEMENT

- You may want to take advantage of community volunteers to enhance your service to constituencies of your mission as a prudent financial management technique.
- Many of the same prudent written hiring, training, supervision, and evaluation human resources policies that a nonprofit organization has in place for its paid staff should be used for effective volunteer

management, including background checks if the organization serves vulnerable population groups.

- Your recruitment and deployment of volunteers should draw upon the diversity of your community and constituencies served by the nonprofit organization's mission.
- You should have a clear distinction between the role of paid staff and volunteers, with adequate supervision of volunteer time and tasks. There should be a description of the scope of the work, necessary skills, expected time commitment, and the impact and benefits of the volunteer's service matched with the volunteer's interests and skills.
- You may want to consider business risk mitigation strategies such as additional insurance coverage specifically related to your use of volunteers.

Partnerships are an excellent vehicle for individuals who want to contribute and combine their particular skill sets to become business owners, sharing both the risks and rewards of the joint project. Partnerships can also be a lucrative investment platform for individuals who can offer investment capital to someone else who brings the actual business expertise. However, there are substantial risks beyond what you contributed to the business for your personal liability involved depending upon the type of partnership and the level of your participation in the operation of the partnership.

In a general partnership, all partners are personally liable for all business debts, including court judgments. Each individual partner can be sued for the full amount of any business debt (though that partner can, in turn, sue the other partners for their share of the debt). There is another option for a limited legal partnership, which may be beneficial.

INSIGHT ON PARTNERSHIPS

INTERVIEW WITH **LAURA YAMANAKA**,

FOUNDER AND CEO OF TEAMCFO

https://nanmckayconnects.com/2020/07/laura-yamanaka/

Laura Yamanaka

Partnerships are like a marriage. If you have a good partnership, it does not mean it's an easy partnership. Two different concepts. If you have a good partnership, it's compounding. Hopefully, you've picked somebody who has complementary skill sets to you. Somebody who has skills, not only from a technical perspective, but an emotional perspective, a risk perspective. It makes you more well-rounded, but doubles, if not more, when you're growing your business.

You cannot be emotionally up all the time. We always had an agreement from the beginning that said somebody had to be positive. We could trade off, but it was the deal that when some things aren't going well and you're going, "Why am I even doing this?" then you had a built-in mechanism for somebody to say, "Okay, let me remind you why we are doing this. And let me remind you of all the successes that we have had," and put things in perspective. It has worked for us. Definitely.

I think that people must have a realistic perspective of what a partnership is. You see people all the time on business shows and television with business partners who go out and get mani-pedis together and everything. No, no, that's not the reality. You want somebody who is going to be working in the business just like you. Maybe in a different aspect. You want somebody who is going to be deadly honest with you. You want somebody you can trust. It's worked out for us. I've been very fortunate.

* * *

The one most important takeaway is to have everything related to the partnership spelled out in as much detail as you possibly can. When you are in the initial throes of developing a partnership, you are excited, and there are blue skies and birds singing. However, if something goes wrong, it can ruin a friendship, a working relationship, and even the business.

Think about who owns the assets of the business. One person may have developed the assets and feel like he or she owns the assets. When the original owner takes on a partner, the partner may feel, because they are a partner, he or she has 50 percent ownership of the assets. Think about how the assets will be divided if you sell. Think about getting a loan. Think about who is going to be in charge of what tasks.

If this agreement is a working partnership, do your skills complement one another's? Everyone is good at something and not good at something else. You want your partner to be good at the things you are not good at.

And you want everything in writing before you sign one single document. Ideally, the document should be reviewed by a separate attorney for each person entering the partnership so you can be advised of your rights and obligations, ensure important understandings and terms are accurately spelled out, and better ensure that each partner walks into the enterprise on a fair footing.

INSIGHTS ON ENTREPRENEURSHIP RELATIONS IN A PARTNERSHIP

INTERVIEW WITH **ROBIN SHAPIRO**,

FOUNDER AND CEO OF HEALTH PERSPECTIVES GROUP AND AUTHOR OF *THE SECRET LANGUAGE OF HEALTH CARE*. ROBIN OBSERVED HER FATHER'S PARTNERSHIPS AND LEARNED VALUABLE LESSONS.

https://nanmckayconnects.com/2021/09/how-to-advocate-for-the-healthcare-you-deserve-robin-shapiro/

Robin Shapiro

My dad also was an entrepreneur. I was super lucky to see his partnerships because he had multiple businesses. Some instances were fantastic. Some instances were terrible. If you are thinking about starting a business, it's good to connect with other people who have been in business and done different arrangements around partnerships. And I am talking about legal partnerships. Understand the pros and cons of doing a partnership 50/50 or a different split. Sometimes there are multiple partners. But from a liability standpoint, a partnership is like a marriage. You have to constantly be attentive to what motivates your partner in a business. I think it is very essential for success, just like in marriage. It doesn't mean that your partner is always going to get what he or she wants, just like in a marriage, but to be tending that need very diligently is essential. On both parts.

A buy–sell agreement when you are in partnership is a critical document that you want to set up in the beginning. Some people say, "Oh, I don't want to mentally think about if things go wrong." That is exactly what you should do. I don't know what the percentage of successful or not successful partnerships is. If you

> *liken it to marriage, it's probably 50/50 at best. I am an optimist. I've been married 25 years, and I have an amazing partner of over 10 years in my first business and I love her, and I love my husband. And we joke that we're spouses all together, but everything is not always roses, just like in a long-term marriage. That's impossible. The real critical thing is, when things are tough and rough and tense and hard, how is it set up? How are you going to be? How are you going to help your partner meet his or her needs as well as your own and make sure that the employees are safe, and your clients are in good shape? That's why they call it work.*

* * *

Developing a partnership agreement is like writing a will. No one wants to think about the downside, only the happy parts. But the minute it gets stormy, or, in the case of the will, someone dies, you want everything spelled out in advance to reduce the conflict that is sure to ensue.

This article may be helpful when you are choosing your legal status: https://investinganswers.com/articles/choosing-your-legal-status-what-kind-business-are-you.

After you have studied the possibilities, you need to know how to apply for that status with your state. The state will have steps for you to follow to establish the business. It starts with formation documentation, and the documentation requirements should be available and typically submittable online. The state department where you obtained information about your domain name is usually the same department to which you submit your formation documents.

I recommend a book entitled *Smooth Sailing: A Practical Guide to Legally Protecting Your Business* by Cheri D. Andrews. She also has courses at https://www.cheriandrews.com/. And I certainly recommend the company that helped me https://nanmckayconnects.com/corpnet

LOCAL REGULATIONS

You may also need to register the business entity with the city in which the business is located (or county if you are in an unincorporated area). The city may have business or occupational license requirements.

INSIGHT INTO THE LOCAL LEGAL ASPECTS

WRITTEN BY **NAN MCKAY**,

FOUNDER AND PRESIDENT OF NAN MCKAY AND ASSOCIATES AND NAN MCKAY CONNECTS, LLC

https://nanmckayconnects.com/in-the-news/

Nan McKay

I had personal experience with this when I moved to California and bought a big house so I could run my business from it, as I had done in Minnesota. I remodeled the garage and two rooms in the house into business space. After about six months, I had a knock on my door. It was the county inspector, who said I could have a business in my house, but I couldn't have any employees unless they were related to me! I had to find and rent a business space and still pay for that big house. We survived, somehow paid for it, and grew. In the long run, because of the growth, we would have had to have found a space to rent anyway, but I didn't anticipate or plan it to have to happen so fast because I had run afoul of a local rule I didn't know about!

* * *

TAX ID NUMBERS

Check out whether you need an IRS Employer Identification Number (EIN) Tax ID Number on this site: https://www.irs-ein-tax-id.com/. An EIN is also known as a federal tax identification number and is used to identify a business entity. You probably will need one. You will need an EIN/Tax ID Number if you fall into any of these categories:

- Started a new business
- Hired or will hire employees, including household employees
- Opened a bank account that requires an EIN for banking purposes
- Need to open a business bank account or want to start a business line of credit
- Changed the legal character or ownership of your organization (for example, you incorporate a sole proprietorship or form a partnership)
- Formed or created a trust, pension plan, corporation, partnership, or LLC
- Represent an estate that operates a business after the owner's death

INTELLECTUAL PROPERTY

Be sure you protect your intellectual property from competitors. Intellectual property includes copyrights, trademarks, patents, and trade secrets—in addition to business property such as equipment. If you have an invention or even a process, you may want or need a patent from the U.S. Patent and Trademark Office (USPTO). Today, you can find information about patents online. Please be aware that the application is typically a long process; plan accordingly for your business time frame.

INSIGHT INTO PROTECTING YOUR ASSETS

INTERVIEW WITH **KARA MAC**,

FOUNDER AND CEO OF KARA MAC SHOES

https://nanmckayconnects.com/2020/05/kara-mac-2/

Kara Mac

Kara Mac, an entrepreneur who spent 25 years of her life as an apparel designer, later followed through with the idea of creating women's shoes that work in every circumstance. She provides invaluable information on patent procedures and expectations.

Not only do I have one patent on my interchangeable shoe heel cover, I got a second patent, which makes it much stronger. That is probably the biggest accomplishment I have had to date. I filed a patent application. They called it a provisional patent in 2013. I had an attorney do it, a friend of somebody I met on the commuter train. He did it during the Super Bowl. I paid him a very little amount of money, and it's usually very expensive to use an attorney to get a patent.

I sent it in and, within one year, it was published. From there, I had another patent attorney take over. There was a ton of back and forth with the U.S. Patent and Trade Organization and to the patent examiners because they would look at the patent and they would reject it. You'd have to redo things and send it to them again. Then they would reject it. This went on for almost four years.

The day I received my first patent was April of 2017. It was so exciting that my attorney came down . . . and hand delivered it to me. He got on a train and hand delivered it to me because it took so long, and it was so difficult. That was an exciting part of my life.

If you have an idea that is very solid and different than anyone else, definitely look into the patenting; whether it's a design, patent, or utility patent, cover yourself. Have nondisclosure agreements prepared for anybody that you're going to be meeting along the path. Be careful where you manufacture, because you never know who wants to take your idea and run with that. And if they have deep pockets and you don't, it doesn't matter. They will squash you.

* * *

INSIGHT INTO PATENTING A COACHING MODEL

INTERVIEW WITH **THRESETTE BRIGGS**,

FOUNDER AND CEO OF PERFORMANCE 3

https://nanmckayconnects.com/2020/06/thresette-briggs/

Thresette Briggs

The reason I got a patent is that I wanted to have a coaching model that was something I owned. There are a lot of coaches. There are a lot of people out there to do coaching, and I respect them all. I wanted to have something I own and could use for people who wanted to accelerate their performance in a profound way and make significant shifts. The model is designed to help them shift a lot faster by looking at various areas that are unique within that model. I decided on a patent because if you are trying to distinguish yourself from everybody who is doing similar things, you are looking at, "What is it that I can do differently, that will compel people to think I am the one they need?" Because my background is in working with companies that were in some sort of survival type of situation like bankruptcy, or a transformation like being cut off by their parent company if they didn't succeed, I had to learn to help people shift into high performance very fast. Because I was in those environments, I learned what was needed to be successful. I decided I can help leaders best by developing a coaching model that helps them do those types of things and sustain them.

* * *

ACTION STEP 18.

COMPLETE YOUR LEGAL STATUS

Use this as a checklist to complete your legal status of the business. Analyze your legal structure alternatives to decide which will best fit your operation. Then make your decisions to get your business underway.

DONE	LEGAL AREA	COMMENTS
	Domain name	
	Business bank account	
	Credit card	
	Legal entity status	
	Local regulations	
	Tax ID numbers	
	Partnership	
	Intellectual property	

CHAPTER 6 TAKEAWAYS

CREATE A LEGAL FRAMEWORK FOR BUSINESS OPERATION

- Create an organizational environment before opening your business doors.
- Transitioning from corporate to solo entrepreneur—consult a business attorney to help you create all the different legal aspects of your business.
- Understanding Benefit Corporation (B Corp) - IRS certification for a business growing in sustainability.
- The benefits of forming business partnerships plus things to keep in mind.
- How to handle entrepreneurial relationships for mutual respect.
- The value of protecting your assets (intellectual properties like copyrights, trademarks, patents, and trade secrets).

CHAPTER 7

CREATE A LEADERSHIP FRAMEWORK TO GUIDE DECISION-MAKING

The leadership framework consists of the administrative plans, policies, procedures, and systems that will establish business parameters and guide business decision-making. The administrative documents, which will provide the framework for your business, will depend somewhat on the type of business you start. The guiding statements that are applicable to all businesses are mission, vision, values, and ethics. The business plan is applicable to all businesses. Operational work systems and culture statements are part of the leadership framework but are more important if your business hires employees.

By creating the documents and status necessary to start the business, you will be required to think about each component part, how they all fit together, and what you want for the outcome of the business. Developing this structure is like building a house. You are not going to move onto an empty lot and set up your bedroom furniture. First, you need the house built so you have a place to put the furniture, and then you move into the house. The components to get into place to establish your business organizational structure include making decisions and then acting to implement your decisions.

MISSION STATEMENT

The mission statement should guide the actions of the organization, spell out its overall goal, provide a sense of direction, and guide decision-making. It provides "the framework or context within which the company's strategies are formulated."[11] A mission statement, a sentence or a short paragraph that defines your entity (what you do), should address who you serve, what you provide, and how you serve them. A mission statement is not a business plan. A mission statement defines why you are doing your business and is an important communication to your staff and the people you work with because it keeps everyone on

11. https://quizlet.com/164671218/strategy-final-chapter-1-tf-flash-cards/#:~:text=The%20final%20component%20of%20the,within%20which%20strategies%20are%20formulated.&text=The%20mission%20of%20a%20company,company%20would%20like%20to%20achieve

the same page in delivering services. The mission statement shows a clear path and motivates a team toward a common goal. These statements are often used in marketing and are often displayed on your website. Your goals should tie back to your mission statement, with your organization's purpose explaining why the organization exists.

A good reference for samples is: https://blog.hubspot.com/marketing/inspiring-company-mission-statements.

Here are a few examples:

- **Life Is Good:** To spread the power of optimism.
- **Sweetgreen:** To inspire healthier communities by connecting people to real food.
- **Patagonia:** Build the best product, cause no unnecessary harm, use business to inspire and implement solutions to the environmental crisis.
- **Nan McKay and Associates:** We deliver innovative solutions for our clientele through professional expertise, collaborative partnerships, and a commitment to customer service.

ACTION STEP 19:

WRITE YOUR MISSION STATEMENT

Answer these questions:

What does your company do?

____

____

How does your company do it?

____

____

Whom do you do it for?

____

____

Why does your company do it? What value are we bringing?

____

____

Now pull it together into a Mission Statement.

____

____

Tailor the mission statement to be very specific. The mission statement should make you feel energized when you read it. Say it out loud, and the statement should roll off your tongue.

VISION STATEMENT

What is the difference between a mission statement and vision statement? A mission statement is for your business today. A vision statement is what it might look like in the future. A mission statement defines the company's business, its objectives, and its approach to reach those objectives. A vision statement describes the desired future position of the company. Elements of mission and vision statements are often combined to provide a statement of the company's purposes, goals, and values.

As an entrepreneur, you should have a clear vision of what you want. Try to think about the details of what this vision looks like. Do you have employees, or are you using contractor platforms? Do you have an office or a storefront? What activities are you involved in? What do you do all day? How do you feel about what you are doing? What do you want this business to look like next year and the year after that? As a founder of the business, think about how your business should work, what your clients will think of the business, and, if you have a product, what that product looks and feels like. If you have a service, how do your clients feel about the timeliness and quality of the service? The more specific you can get about your vision, the easier it will be to set your direction and the clearer the picture will be for the people who work with you.

Having a vision and general roadmap is an effective way to ensure your goals are clearly stated and met. You will probably have to adjust your vision along the way. Perfectly normal. As the Cheshire Cat once said to Alice, "If you don't know where you are going, it doesn't matter which path you take." The people you work with will be more inclined to follow you if you know what you want to achieve. Once you have the notes of your vision written down, the next step is to write a vision statement for your business.

A vision statement is a vivid, idealized description of a desired outcome that inspires, energizes, and helps you create a mental picture of what you want your organization to be. A vision statement defines the way an organization will look in the future and tells what you want your business to be, but not how you are going to get there. The vision statement is your dream, so project five years into the future focusing on success.

Examples:

- **Teach for America:** One day, all children in this nation will have the opportunity to attain an excellent education.
- **Creative Commons:** Realizing the full potential of the internet—universal access to research and education, full participation in culture—to drive a new era of development, growth, and productivity.
- **Nan McKay and Associates:** We deliver premier business solutions and strategies to strengthen neighborhoods nationwide.

ACTION STEP 20.

WRITE YOUR VISION STATEMENT

What are your hopes and dreams?

____

____

What problems are we solving for the greater good?

____

____

Who are we inspiring?

____

____

What does success look like?

____

____

What will the business look like in three years? Five years?

____

____

Now pull it all into a vision statement.

____

____

ACTION STEP 21.

MISSION AND VISION STATEMENTS

The stated mission and vision should be the major factors that affect everything the organization does. All policy and operating decisions should be made within the context of how they relate to the mission and vision. The mission is to know who you are and the vision is to know where you're going. The mission is today and what we do. The vision focuses on tomorrow and what we want to become.

Mission: ______________________________

Vision: ______________________________

Why It Works: ______________________________

Examples of Mission and Vision Statements from Clear Voice:[12]

Company: TED

Mission: Spread ideas.

Vision: We believe passionately in the power of ideas to change attitudes, lives and, ultimately, the world.

Why it works: The TED mission to "spread ideas" is a simple demonstration of how they serve. The vision is all about impact, how spreading ideas invokes change in the world.

Company: LinkedIn

Mission: To connect the world's professionals to make them more productive and successful.

12. https://www.clearvoice.com/

Vision: To create economic opportunity for every member of the global workforce.

Why it works: LinkedIn succinctly captures what they do (connect) and who they serve (the world's professionals) in their mission. The vision encompasses every working person in the world.

VALUES STATEMENT

Writing out your core values or principles helps you make decisions. The values will guide others who work with you to perform their work. There are usually three types of values: personal, professional, and social. Personal values are those values you hold dear to you, like integrity and determination. Professional values reflect on your personal values, such as adhering to rules and regulations and self-determination work environments. Social values are how you give back to shape society. Social values can range from creating products and services benefitting society to supporting and investing in social causes dear to your heart. For example, if you work in a governmental environment, you know that integrity and adhering to rules and regulations are extremely important, especially when it is an area influenceable by corruption. Your social values might include allowing staff to volunteer to run a coat drive in the winter for the people you serve.

Your corporate values should all be in alignment for business success. For example, if your personal value is to win, then your professional value might be "win at all costs." How do you think these line up with social values? They probably don't.

Values affect communication and employee engagement. Values shape the work environment and business decisions.

ACTION STEP 22.

SELECT YOUR VALUES

Under the section "Ours," put a check mark if you want to adopt the value shown. Then decide whether the value would be a personal, professional, or social value for your business. Add other values you would like to include and categorize them.

OURS	VALUE	PERSONAL	PROFESSIONAL	SOCIAL
	Integrity			
	Commitment to customers			
	Quality			
	Performance excellence			
	Boldness			
	Honesty			
	Trust			
	Accountability			
	Fun			
	Passion			

ETHICS STATEMENT

Ethics has become one of today's most critical business concerns. You may not think that concerns about ethics are applicable to your business, but the facts are that there are serious consequences in the public and private sector for failing to take concrete, specific measures to ensure that your business practices and personnel follow the appropriate ethical guidelines and responsibilities. It is imperative that your organization avoid actions and decisions that lead to inquiries involving ethical or legal improprieties.

Ethics refers to a system of moral principles or values, the rules or standards governing the conduct of the members of a profession, or the accepted principles of right and wrong. In simple terms, ethics means doing what is right, fair, honest, and legal. For the most part, businesses and most people who work in them are being fair, honest, and trying to do the right thing. Each of us has a significant responsibility to act ethically. The actions we take, the decisions we make, and the daily behaviors we exhibit will all ultimately determine how our organizations are judged. When it comes to ethics, we are all responsible.

Create an ethical culture. Communicate your ethics policy clearly to your employees and clients. An ethics policy is also an effective way of demonstrating a corporate commitment to honest and proper business practices, from the way that an organization treats its employees to how it deals with its environmental impact. Generally, a code of ethics policy should state that you expect an employee to be honest, trustworthy, loyal, respectful, responsible, fair, kind, competent and accountable, and law abiding. In addition, ensure that your business celebrates diversity, teamwork, green practices, and proper dress codes. As the owner of the company, you must act ethically as the leader to demonstrate this value in how you interact with your staff, vendors, and the public. The boss must "walk the walk," not just "talk the talk."

If you have an office or storefront, post your ethics statement, a clear statement synthesizing your policy, around the office and distribute the policy to employees. Address ethical issues at meetings when relevant, and reward ethical behavior. Ask people to talk about examples of different ethical dilemmas or decisions. Review the rules and the reasons for them. Make it clear that you will not tolerate unethical conduct and outline the consequences for noncompliance.

Being ethical is challenging. The first challenge is knowing the right thing to do. However, even if you know what you should do, the second and more difficult challenge is doing the right thing. The third challenge is to manage competing "rights," and the fourth and final challenge is to remember that everything counts.

Most of us learned the difference between right and wrong at a young age. We learned that honesty is good, lying is bad, earning is good, and stealing is bad. This knowledge allowed us to separate good from bad and right from wrong. As we moved through our lives, we found others had different ideas about right and wrong, and we probably encountered a good number of temptations to test our own character and values as well. Most of us probably found that as we get older, the less clearly right or wrong things seem. Sometimes "the right thing" is obvious, and sometimes it is not. We need guidelines to help us.

We can often rely on two kinds of "laws" that can be applied at work. The first category includes common restrictions "everyone knows" (e.g., one shouldn't steal from, assault, or slander another person). The second category relates to business in general. Examples of business ethics would be included in areas such as procurement, labor or hiring practices, misuse or improper disclosure of proprietary information, and discrimination.

Ignorance of a law is not an acceptable excuse for breaking the law. Consider not only the actual words and provisions of the laws but also the probable intentions behind the words. Forgetting the intention of the law often leads to manipulating the law to justify your actions.

We all make promises or commitments, as members of an organization, and as individuals. We make those commitments to our employees, colleagues, clients, and superiors. A good guideline for knowing what's right or ethical is to live up to your promises or commitments. If you take on a project or task with a deadline, the commitment is that you will complete the project on time. If you accept a position at a higher level within an organization, chances are the job comes with a higher level of responsibility. By accepting the position, you commit to fulfilling the responsibilities.

Remember that ethical behavior is a personal choice. If something feels wrong, the reality is that it probably is wrong.

We have provided an example, but you should make up your own. You should also get legal advice where needed.

Example of an Ethics Code:

> Our employee code of ethics and business conduct outlines our expectations regarding the behavior of our employees toward other members, customers, stakeholders, and society.
>
> Our company stands for the core values of synergy, honesty, and integrity. As such, we expect all organization members to be directed by the same values in their judgment and behavior.
>
> Open communication and expression should be guided by the desire for a respectful, safe, and collaborative working environment.
>
> **Scope**
> This policy applies to all organizational members regardless of rank or employment type.

Compliance with law

Employees must work to protect the company and its legal interests by complying with all environmental, trading, safety, and privacy laws.

Safety in the working environment

All employees should respect their colleagues, supervisors, and customers. Any discriminatory behavior or harassment will not be tolerated.

Professionalism

Employees must show integrity and professionalism in every aspect of conduct, including matters involving absenteeism, tardiness, and dress code compliance. Personal appearance should project the company's commitment to professionalism.

Integrity

All employees should fulfill their work with integrity and respect toward our stakeholders. Members are discouraged from accepting gifts from clients or partners for the benefit of another party. We are all expected to avoid any personal, financial, or other interests that may interfere with the quality of work.

Care for the physical environment

Employees should treat company property and their physical environment with respect and care.

Disciplinary actions

Employees who repeatedly or deliberately fail to follow our code of conduct will meet an appropriate disciplinary action.

Following a clear warning, employees who persistently show indecorous behavior may face demotion, reprimand, detraction of benefits, suspension, or termination.

Legal actions may be taken in cases of theft, embezzlement, corruption, and other unlawful actions.

Your ethics statement could include a code of conduct. There are many templates online that will help you create your own.

ORGANIZATIONAL CULTURE STATEMENT

Culture is the personality of the organization. The assumptions, values, norms, style, tangible signs, and behaviors of personnel are indicators of your organizational culture. The organizational culture has a direct effect on how people relate to each other and how they perform and may also have a major effect on employee satisfaction and retention.

Organizational culture is a term that is difficult to express but one that everyone recognizes and can describe within each work environment. Visible expressions of organizational culture can be found in how the office facility is arranged and decorated, the clothing worn, the organizational processes and structures, the way clients are treated, and the general way people go about everyday activities in the organization. Other examples of culture can be found not only in value statements and priorities but also in commonly used language, logos, brochures, company slogans, and employee perks such as cars, window offices, parking spaces, and titles. Culture is often defined by what management rewards.

Organizational culture is important because understanding and assessing the organizational culture can mean the difference between success and failure in today's environment.

You and other senior leaders of the organization define the culture. Good cultures are supportive of excellence, teamwork, honesty, customer service orientation, and pride in one's work. Your culture statement ties in to the mission, vision, and value statements—all of which set the standard for how your company will impact the workplace. With a culture statement, like ethics, you cannot just talk the talk; you must walk the walk to ensure the culture statement matches the actual work environment.

A sample culture statement might be:

Integrity
Our relationships, work, and decisions are guided by honesty and a commitment to strong moral character. We are transparent in our actions and hold ourselves to the highest ethical standards.

Collaboration
We are one team, passionate about our company and the work we do. We believe that diversity is our strength and work together to achieve goals for our customers and ourselves.

Leadership
Our reputation for excellence is built on a foundation of experience and expert knowledge. We value innovation and learning, leveraging both to deliver excellence to our clients while remaining at the forefront of our industry.

Trust
Strong relationships are the core of our business. We are reliable, dependable, and objective in our interactions with customers, partners, and team members.

Quality
A job well done is our greatest reward, and we funnel our passion into every project. Through tenacity and a commitment to excellence, we deliver a product to be proud of, every time.

INSIGHTS ON CULTURE AND LEADERSHIP STYLE

INTERVIEW WITH **CLARE PRICE**,

FOUNDER AND CEO OF OCTAIN GROWTH, AND AUTHOR OF *MAKING REMOTE WORK*

https://nanmckayconnects.com/2021/01/clare-price-podcast/.

Clare Price

Clare Price is CEO of a global strategic planning consultancy that helps small and mid-market companies grow to dominate their markets by fueling the speed of business using the six key business accelerators: product service development, customer acquisition, branding, positioning, marketing, and sales.

If you have a strong company culture, if people understand the values of the company, if they are all rowing the boat the same way, they will be more productive, they will be much better employees. Creating that company culture is critical.

The second thing is leadership communication. You have your culture, and you have your vision. Communication is tricky, particularly remotely. One of my friends said, "I have no idea what to do with my people. I'm used to managing by walking around, and I can't do that anymore. What do I do?" Managers must cultivate a new leadership style that incorporates being able to communicate across the world, across state lines, whatever.

The other thing, in addition to culture, is structure—having a structure within your company as to how you are going to work. How you want people to communicate is critical. I have seen two things with clients. I have seen clients who trust their people completely, sort of throw them in the pool and see if they can swim. And that can lead to a feeling of being isolated, a feeling of being overwhelmed, a feeling of not sure what to do next, particularly for those who are used to a little bit more formal structure. So that's one end of the scale.

On the other end of the scale, I have a client who is complaining to me that her boss wants her to check in every twenty minutes to make sure that she is on task, and that she is getting things done. She says, "I can't get things done when he is calling me every twenty minutes." You need a happy medium here. You have to be able to have that leadership, have confidence in your employees, but also have a well-described process and structure that the individuals can all understand, and people can follow.

* * *

ENSURING A CULTURE OF DIVERSITY AND INCLUSION

Diversity, equality, and inclusion (DEI) has become a buzzword for ensuring that your workplace is a healthy, supportive, fair, equitable, and inclusive environment for all. It means acknowledging white privilege and the legacy of racism and using the available tools to constantly review and critique your company and its practices to ensure it is in alignment.

Far more than the annual training of staff required by most companies, DEI needs to be ingrained into all of the management functions—including, but not limited to, hiring, training, promotion, directing, controlling, and firing—and imbedded within the culture.

Diversity is often perceived to be about perspective, representation, tough conversation, and supporting inclusion. Inclusion prompts answers about creating environments conducive to feedback, supporting diversity, and being open. Equity is described as fairness, sameness, and valuing diversity and inclusion. Diversity refers to all the many ways that people differ, and equity is about creating fair access, opportunity, and advancement for all those different people.

INSIGHTS ON DEI IN BUSINESS

INTERVIEW WITH **CATHY LIGHT**,

FOUNDER AND CEO OF LIDERANCA GROUP

https://nanmckayconnects.com/2020/12/increase-performance-with-dei-podcast-cathy-light/

Cathy Light

Liderança Group introduced a unique, metrics-driven roadmap for driving diversity, equity, and inclusion (DEI) in the workplace, helping leaders identify opportunities for improvement, elevate conversations around diversity, and inspire change. *Insights Success* magazine selected **Cathy Light** as one of the top ten most successful women in cloud entrepreneurs.

When I look at workplace diversity, it's about a range of differences within a company, or workforce, particularly related to the categories around gender, race, ethnicity, age, and sexual orientation. And that's important. We need to look around us and see that we are incorporating diversity in hiring, having those differences, create collaboration, create differences of opinion.

Workplace diversity is key. When I look at equality in the workplace, we really need to make sure that people are given equal opportunities, equal pay, and are well accepted for their differences. People want to be able to share who they are and not have to be scared to do so.

Equality in the workplace is really creating that inclusive and conducive work environment where all employees feel safe, secure, happy, and can thrive. In our workplace, it should be a lot easier than it is.

It is systemic around good leadership practices. It is the act of ensuring that all people, regardless of their identity, are given the same rights and opportunities within a company, ensuring that you offer them safety, secure employment, advancement, opportunities, and experiences.

I look at inclusiveness as being able to have a voice in your organization to be heard, to feel connected. That openness needs to provide that when you have meetings, look around the room. Who is speaking? If someone is not speaking up, then it is up to us as leaders to ask them in a respectful way, "What are you thinking? What's your opinion?" It is not putting them on the spot but being just open or perhaps having a conversation afterwards.

Another important part of this connectedness is to sit down with your employees and have a coffee talk. Have a one-on-one conversation where you ask them simply, "How are you doing? Is there anything I can help you with? How can I help you enjoy your job more? What resources can I provide you to make you more successful?" Those are just simple conversations that should not be difficult but are extremely important in the workplace."

* * *

A solo entrepreneur can apply this DEI advice to themselves and their business in how they reach out to their potential customer base to present their product/services to all by having DEI as part of their outreach and marketing strategy. As the solo entrepreneur begins the hiring process, they can create work practices such as periodic anonymous surveys or hiring an outside DEI specialist to review and assess the company's work environment and culture.

ACTION STEP 23.

WRITE A CULTURE STATEMENT THAT INCLUDES DIVERSITY, EQUITY, AND INCLUSION (DEI)

Review the information on diversity, equity, and inclusion to ensure your culture statement effectively conveys your commitment to DEI.

____

____

____

BUSINESS PLAN

A business plan is highly desirable because it requires research and decision-making on such critical elements as your market, competition, business model, and even on some of the regulatory constraints. If you are going to seek capital, either venture capital or a loan, these institutions will require you to present a business plan. Additionally, you must know where you are going, or you will never get there!

A business plan is central to how you start, grow, and develop your business. I have prepared my own business plans for various enterprises and would highly recommend attending your local Small Business Association (SBA) trainings on how to prepare a business plan. I also highly recommend accessing a free Senior Corps of Retired Executives (SCORE) consultant through the SBA! You can request one specialized in your industry and, with their experience, they usually provide excellent advice!

The U.S. Small Business Administration provides five reasons you need a business plan:

1. **It will help you steer your business as you start and grow.**
   Think of a business plan as a GPS to get your business going. A good business plan guides you through each stage of starting and managing your business. You'll use your business plan like a GPS for how to structure, run, and grow your new business. A business plan is a way to think through and detail all the key elements of how your business will run.

2. **It's not as hard as you think.**
   A business plan is a written tool about your business that projects three to five years ahead and outlines the path your business intends to take to make money and grow revenue. Think of it as a living project for your business and not as a one-time document. Break it down into mini-plans—one for sales and marketing, one for pricing, one for operations, and so on.

3. **It will help you to reach business milestones.**
   A well-thought-out business plan helps you to step back and think objectively about the key elements of your business and informs your decision-making as you move forward. Your plan is essential whether you need to secure a business loan or not. Keep in mind that the plan does not have to be like an encyclopedia and does not have to have all the answers.

4. **It can help you get funding.**
   Business plans can help you get funding or bring on new business partners. Having one in place will help investors feel confident that they will see a return on their investment. Your business plan is the tool you will use to persuade others that working with you (or investing in your business) is a smart decision.

5. **There's no wrong way to write a business plan.**
   Business plans can be written in a variety of ways, from a robust document to a one-page plan. You can pick a plan format that works best for you. What is important is your business plan meets your needs. Most business plans fall into one of two common categories: traditional or lean startup.

Traditional business plans are more common, use a standard structure, and encourage you to go into detail in each section. Traditional plans tend to require more work upfront. Lean startup business plans are less common but still use a standard structure. They focus on summarizing only the most important points of the key elements of your plan. They can take as little as one hour to make and are typically just one page.

INSIGHTS ON WRITING A BUSINESS DESCRIPTION AND PLAN

INTERVIEW WITH **SUSIE CARDER**,

FOUNDER AND CEO OF SUSAN CARDER PROFIT COACH AND AUTHOR OF *POWER YOUR PROFITS*

https://nanmckayconnects.com/2021/04/how-to-take-your-business-from-10k-to-10-million-susie-carder/

Susie Carder

Susie Carder is a woman of power. She gives you the formula, the mindset, and the tools to make your business a success.

The first thing we all need to do everybody resists doing. You've got to put that plan together. You must get it out of your head. I think if people took the time to put their business plan together to map it out, they would see if it is going to be viable. Or is it not viable, because a lot of times we start a business, and we pull our pricing out of our hiney. We are making stuff up without really looking at

"Is this viable?" The first thing is getting it all out of your head and get it on paper. It doesn't have to be perfect. It's just for you and your internal team.

* * *

Susie Carder (https://susiecarder.com/) has a free ten-point Business Planning Assessment.

When you are starting up, your business will probably take twists and turns until you establish where you want to be. Be sure your plan is clear and keep your plan updated, making revisions as you go along. It will assist you in so many ways, such as writing a business description, bringing clarity to your own mind, and further defining your mission and vision. In fact, your mission statement should be included in your plan.

To start your own business plan, I recommend starting with some internet searching to find sample business plans specific for the industry you want to join. For example, if you enter "Business Plan Template" into a Google search coupled with the type of industry you are seeking, you will find quite a few free templates, which will help you with your business plan.

Because knowing where to start can be challenging, the SBA has tools to help make writing a business plan less intimidating and time-consuming. The SBA offers a Business Plan Tool that helps simplify the process. The tool consists of eight easy-to-follow steps to help create a well-prepared plan. SBA has a template, (https://www.score.org/resource/business-plan-template-startup-business), but it also has two other resources: a business plan course and free consulting services through SCORE (Senior Corp of Retired Executives), which I have used twice and highly recommend.

A business plan usually includes these parts:

- Executive Summary
- Company Description
- Products and Services
- Marketing Plan
- Operational Plan
- Management and Organization
- Startup Expenses and Capitalization
- Financial Plan
- Appendices

To learn more about putting your business plan together, go to the SBA's online Learning Center and take the self-paced course, How to Write a Business Plan. The course explains the importance of business planning, describes the components of a plan, and provides access to resources and sample plans. You can also look at the SBA's Business Planning Guide for more information and to view business plan templates.

If you want a more hands-on approach, you can get assistance from an SBA resource partner to help complete your business plan. Working with a mentor or counselor from SCORE, a Small Business Development Center, or a Women's Business Center can help with all aspects of starting, growing, or expanding your business.

ACTION STEP 24.

QUICK-START BUSINESS PLAN

The Company

- Business sector
- Company goals and objectives
- Company ownership structure
- Ownership background
- Company management structure
- Company assets
- Location of your operation

The Product or Services

- Product or services description
- Product patents, if any
- Future products or services

Marketing and Sales Strategy

- Target market
- Established customers
- Pricing
- Advertising
- Social media
- Market research findings

Competitor Analysis

- The competitors and their competitive advantage

SWOT Analysis

- Strengths
- Weaknesses
- Opportunities
- Threats

Management and Organizational Structure

- Organizational structure
- Staffing
- Suppliers

Capital Requirements

Financial Projections

Executive Summary

OPERATIONAL WORK SYSTEMS

Standards not only include your mission, vision, and core values but they also include your operational work systems, including your policies and procedures for how work is accomplished.

Policies: When your business includes employees, you should have written policies on these areas:

- Social Media Policy
- Privacy Policy
- Diversity, Equality, and Inclusion (DEI) Policy
- Employee Policy
- Leave of Absence Policy

If you have products to sell, you should have a written Payment and Refund Policy.

Work Systems: The term *work systems* refers to the way in which an organization aligns its internal operations and workforce with its key vendors, suppliers, partners, and collaborators to provide a quality and cost-effective service to its clients. Work systems include your communication protocol, your expectations, and your tracking mechanisms between your internal work processes and your external resources necessary to plan and deliver your services to your customers. Decisions on work systems are very strategic for the organization. The decisions involve the best ways to provide services to our clients with the highest level of quality, customer service, and cost efficiencies.

Work Processes: Work processes, a subset of your overall work systems, refers to everything that happens (all the activities) within a work system. The term *process* refers to linked or coordinated activities with the purpose of producing a result (or service) for an internal or external customer. Generally, processes involve combinations of people, machines, tools, techniques, or materials in a defined series of steps or actions. In some situations, processes might require adherence to a specific sequence of steps, with documentation (sometimes formal) of procedures and requirements, including well-defined measurement and control steps.

Work processes create the internal structure of how the work is accomplished and involve all the activities needed to sustain the various operational functions. Work processes involve how staff is used and which tools should be created to accomplish the work. Examples of work processes include written procedures for the functional areas of the program, mini procedures for a specific task, workflows, automated reports, meetings, and checklists. Work processes should be easy to reference, simple to understand, be designed in a step-by-step process, and tie into procedure checklists. The more workers you have involved in the business, the more these tools are needed.

Projects are unique work processes intended to produce an outcome and then go out of existence. The primary benefit of effective work processes in your day-to-day operation ensures consistency in operations, high-quality control results, and more productivity because staff has needed resources.

Procedures: Written procedures are essential to ensure consistency in operations. Errors and frustration are greatly reduced if your people know what to do, when to do it, and how to do it. In addition, the sustainability of your organization greatly increases because there will be a roadmap for all future staff to follow.

Even if you are a solo entrepreneur, I recommend having procedures in place. Procedures are critical for business continuity and sustainability. If you utilize contractors or freelancers, people need to know what your expectations are for how work is to be accomplished. If you are absent for any reason, and especially in an emergency, you want others to be able to step in and do the work that is necessary. Without written procedures, even well-meaning people will not know what to do.

The difference between a policy and a procedure is that policies are words of direction created to ensure and support key requirements, mission, or vision. Procedures are documented actions to be taken to show how the policy is incorporated into daily operations. Policies may not always have supported procedures, but procedures should always support a policy (and may support many policies).

Good procedures include the following:

- The specific tasks to be accomplished
- Designation of responsible staff
- Time frames in which tasks must be performed (if applicable)
- The appropriate forms, documents, and systems to be used

- Approvals (if necessary)
- Regulatory or administrative plan references as applicable

A single procedure could involve multiple tasks.

Below are some tips for writing a procedure:

- A procedure is a set of instructions that outlines the steps for performing a task(s).
- A procedure should tell someone how to do something, not just what to do.
- A procedure breaks a task or tasks into discrete, sequential steps.
- A procedure uses short, active voice/action statements. "Make three copies" is better than "should make three copies."
- A procedure includes time frames and document expectations, when appropriate. These can include signatures, copies of forms, case notes, and the like.
- Finally, testing the procedures before fully implementing them and getting feedback from staff that uses them is important.

Work Process Tools: As part of the work systems and processes, tools will further ensure that the work to be done is being accomplished in a timely manner. Once we have work processes and tools in place, we can measure progress. These tools could take many forms such as calendars, software tracking systems, and file systems. The tools function as part of our leadership system to ensure consistency in operation so that timely results are achieved.

Sustainability: The term *sustainability* refers to your organization's ability to address current business needs and to have the agility and strategic management to prepare successfully for your future business and operating environment. Both external and internal factors need to be considered. Sustainability considerations might include workforce capability and capacity, resource availability, technology, knowledge, core competencies, work systems, facilities, and equipment. Sustainability might be affected by changes in the marketplace, changes in the legal and regulatory environment, or unexpected turnover of key personnel. In addition, sustainability has a component related to day-to-day preparedness for real-time or short-term emergencies. Sustainability over time will fall back on the work systems and work processes you have in place. These systems may have to be tweaked but having them in place ensures that whoever is operating your business has a clear direction for the quality and quantity of work to be done within a specified time frame.

ACTION STEP 25.

OPERATIONAL WORK SYSTEMS

I will need a policy for these areas:

- ☐ Social Media Policy
- ☐ Privacy Policy
- ☐ Diversity, Equality, and Inclusion (DEI) Policy
- ☐ Employee Policy
- ☐ Leave of Absence Policy
- ☐ Payment and Refund Policy
- ☐ Other: ________________________________

I will need procedures in these areas to clarify how I want the work accomplished:

____

____

I will need these types of work process tools:

____

____

CHAPTER 7 TAKEAWAYS

CREATE A LEADERSHIP FRAMEWORK TO GUIDE DECISION-MAKING

- Develop a structure of operational work systems and culture statements.
- Write your mission statement to guide the actions of your organization.
- Define communication between you, your staff, and other people you work with.
- Write your vision statement to effectively ensure your goals are clearly stated and met.
- Have three types of values statements: personal, professional, and social.
- Have an ethics statement to govern the conduct of your organization and its stakeholders.
- Understand the value of a strong organizational culture statement.
- Explore how to ingrain diversity, equity, and inclusion (DEI) into all of the management functions.
- Write a culture statement that includes the four pillars of DEI.
- Utilize the power of a business plan in starting, growing, and developing a business.
- Explore tips on how to approach writing an effective business description and plan.
- Understand how to develop standards that include operational work systems.

CHAPTER 8

ESTABLISH FINANCIAL SYSTEMS FOR BUSINESS STABILITY

STARTUP CAPITAL

If you wait until you are ready to leave your current job before starting your entrepreneurship, a direct pivot can be risky. Something must happen fast if you do not have enough cash to cover your personal and business expenses for about twelve months.

Three ways to mitigate the risk include procuring a contract before you leave, taking on the business as a side hustle in addition to your work career, and having a twelve-month cash reserve. How far you can delve into your business "on the side" while you are employed depends on your bandwidth of time available.

If you can procure a limited, manageable project before you leave that allows you to get your sea legs (e.g., offering the product/service on a small scale to someone who is familiar with your knowledge and skills), you will mitigate the risk because you are starting your business with a contract in place.

The contact for the contract/first project is usually based on someone you are in contact with stemming from your current employment. If you can line up a good contract prior to leaving your job without crossing any legal or integrity boundaries, it is the best of all worlds. But be careful of any potential conflicts of interest, especially if you signed a conflict-of-interest agreement when you were hired.

INSIGHTS ON STARTUP MONEY

INTERVIEW WITH **ROBIN SHAPIRO**,

FOUNDER AND CEO OF HEALTH PERSPECTIVES GROUP AND AUTHOR OF THE *SECRET LANGUAGE OF HEALTH CARE*

https://nanmckayconnects.com/2021/09/how-to-advocate-for-the-healthcare-you-deserve-robin-shapiro/

Robin Shapiro

I looked at my savings. I looked at my severance. And we were very fortunate in that we had health care for a year as part of my severance agreement. That safety net was mentally critical. I basically looked at what I needed. I said, "Okay, I'm going to give it a year. And if it doesn't work out, I'll do something else." On the second day I was in business, I had a former colleague call and say, "Hey, I heard you're starting this business and a client called and they want what you did previously. Would you give them a call?" Sometimes the stars align like that, and the business grew from there.

* * *

INTERVIEW WITH **KARLENE HIBBERT**, FOUNDER AND CEO OF ONYX MARKETING

https://nanmckayconnects.com/2021/10/how-to-pivot-from-nursing-to-tech-marketing-karlene-hibbert/

Karlene Hibbert

Karlene Hibbert is the founder of Onyx Marketing Mix, a webinar funnel boutique helping entrepreneurs increase their conversions without increasing their ad spend.

If you are going to quit your job and start a business, I would say, "Great, congratulations, great, fantastic." But I would also say to make sure you have at least six months' worth of salary put aside, maybe even six months to a year. If you can set salary aside, there isn't so much pressure. These are the things that I wish I had done beforehand.

These are things I have learned, because you learn as you go along. And you learn by your—I was going to say mistakes, but they are not mistakes. They are opportunities to learn. Work out how much money you will need to survive for six months and work out how many clients you will need to survive those six months or the six months beyond.

Then put a plan in place to actually get those clients so that you are not pressured thinking of where the next penny is going to come from. What you find is, when you're so excited about what it is you do, you just jump in, and then you do it. You do have to prepare for it.

* * *

INTERVIEW WITH **ROBIN BREWTON**

https://nanmckayconnects.com/2022/01/how-to-pivot-into-entrepreneurship-without-fear-robin-brewton/

Robin Brewton

In one of my past careers, I was a financial advisor. I'm not going to offer advice, but I have a securities license, a series 65, and I always tell people, You need a minimum of six months of savings accumulated to start your business if you're going to take a leap. You need at least that and probably a year.

* * *

In some circumstances, people can't wait that long—for example, if you have created a new widget and you believe the market is just right. You feel you must capitalize on that, and you may need to dip into your savings a little bit. I don't like to recommend that. But be sure you have saved six to twelve months' salary before you leap.

We are talking about both personal and business expenses when we calculate how much to save and over what period. The good news is, at least from my own experience, for so many of us who are starting a new career or twilight career, a second career late in our lives, the costs are minimal.

There are not as many business expenses as we might think, particularly if we can do something online. A lot of what we need is simply our own expertise, our passion, our network, a telephone, and maybe a website.

INSIGHTS INTO HAVING MULTIPLE REVENUE STREAMS

INTERVIEW WITH **LESLIE ANDRACHUK**,

FOUNDER AND CEO OF ALPHA WOMAN COMPANY AND ALPHA WOMAN PODCAST

https://nanmckayconnects.com/2021/10/how-alpha-woman-empowers-women-leslie-andrachuk/

Leslie Andrachuk

Leslie Andrachuk is a global digital publishing and marketing executive who pivoted to founding Alpha Woman, a multiplatform media company, with the mission to help women be their best—physically, mentally, and professionally.

As an entrepreneur, I have made it my business in these first few years to make sure that I have multiple revenue streams so that I can pay my mortgage, make sure that my family is fed. Even from a personal standpoint. I started my business with a partner. We bootstrapped this business; we have put in our time and our personal money. I am a single parent. I don't have a huge financial runway, and I didn't at the time. I personally had to have a side hustle. I have a marketing consulting company. And I help companies with their marketing on the side, so that I can personally pay my bills. Alpha Woman, three years later, is a full-time business. But in those early years, when I left my full-time job, I made sure that I maintained that marketing consulting company for a couple years, just to make sure. Thank goodness I did, because during COVID, most of our revenue projections were based on our events. That was our revenue strategy for 2020. I had a full-day, Alpha Woman Entrepreneur Conference organized for March 20. You can guess what happened. Thankfully, I did have these other ways to create revenue for me personally, as I dealt *with what was happening with the business. Other people might have $200,000 in their savings account that they can apply to their business. I didn't.*

* * *

INSIGHTS ON MAKING A PROFIT

INTERVIEW WITH **SUSIE CARDER**,

AUTHOR OF *POWER YOUR PROFITS: LEARN HOW TO TAKE YOUR BUSINESS FROM $10,000 TO $10 MILLION*

https://nanmckayconnects.com/2021/04/how-to-take-your-business-from-10k-to-10-million-susie-carder/

Susie Carder

First is the business plan. The second thing is to put a forecast together. Math is money, and money is fun.

In my book, I give you a forecast. I give you a pricing formula to how to price your services so you're not in the dark anymore. I quit making business decisions based on feelings. Feelings have nothing to do with business. It's a different side of your brain that you have to look at logically and then look at your purpose.

What do I need to do to make the impact I need to make in the world so I can pay myself to continue to make the impact that I'm making in the world? We must do that with our financial well-being. We can't all do this for free. Now, if you're a philanthropist, do it for free, good for you. But most of us can't.

I can't afford to do what I do for free. I must make a living to provide for my family, to provide for myself, to provide for my future. It is fiscally responsible to make a profit. It's your expectation to make a profit.

Profit is not the luxury profit, not what's left over. It's like savings. There's never any money left over to save, right? It must be planned for. I want you to put your business plan together, and then go directly to Chapter 8 of my book, which is the money chapter.

* * *

VENTURE CAPITAL

Women in venture capital, or VC, are investors who provide venture capital funding to startups. Women make up a small (usually less than 10 percent) fraction of the venture capital private equity workforce. Venture capitalists look for a competitive advantage in the market. They want their portfolio companies to be able to generate sales and profits before competitors enter the market and reduce profitability. The fewer direct competitors operating in the space, the better.

INSIGHTS ON VENTURE CAPITAL FUNDING

INTERVIEW WITH **BRIANNA MCDONALD,**

PRESIDENT OF THE NORTHWEST REGION OF THE KEIRETSU FORUM

https://nanmckayconnects.com/2021/04/invest-in-and-support-women-brianna-mcdonald/

Brianna McDonald

Brianna McDonald is president of the Northwest & Rockies Region of the Keiretsu Forum investor network, the largest and most active venture investor globally, comprising over fifty chapters with over 3,000 active members investing more than $450 million into over 600 companies.

There are many different players in the entrepreneurial ecosystem. There are other funders at different stages. There are true angels out there who will write checks for individuals at the conceptualization or ideation stage of a company, when it is just an idea on a napkin. Other organizations will help fund after the idea has been baked a little bit, but now they need to build a product and get that done.

Then there is us—after they have completed the products and they have a little bit of revenue, and they need to scale up the business. They need more marketing dollars; they need to hire a bigger team; they need to bring on more expertise and get into new regions. That is when they would come to us when they need that.

Many of our customers are serial entrepreneurs. They have built and sold companies before. They understand that fundraising is a second full-time job in addition to growing your business. Streamlining that fundraising process is essential. Because if they're able to close the funding dollars in a reasonable time, they can get back to doing what they do best, which is growing the business.

It is like going to the bank, but in a different way. When you go to a bank, you typically must put up collateral. These are individuals you are meeting, a community, and people doing business with people they know and trust. I am essentially betting on the CEO to execute and do what they say. I believe in people and innovation. I am assuming that they will be able to do something someday to make the world better.

I typically get equity in the company. I will get stock. I get paper that will hopefully one day turn into something I see that is very interesting. If it is a convertible note, that is essentially more of a debt-financing tool, and I'll get an interest rate. I will usually get a discount on the valuation when they go toward the equity round. I believe that the entrepreneur will hit their milestones, convert their notes, and then get me that equity at that discounted valuation. The debt converts if the company fails before it is converted. I am a little bit more secured in my investment because I do have that little 5 or 7 percent interest that I've been carrying on the cash I put in over the time on the note.

* * *

Women entrepreneurs have traditionally not been the primary targets of venture capitalists, but that is changing, according to CNBC, with more money going to female startups.[13] Spurred by racial injustice and the impact of the COVID pandemic, venture capitalists are opening more opportunities for diverse founders.

13. CNBC https://www.cnbc.com/2021/11/18/female-founded-start-ups-see-funding-increase-in-2021-.html

INSIGHTS INTO ACCELERATORS

INTERVIEW WITH **DR. SILVIA MAH**,

SPEAKER, INVESTOR, AND PODCAST HOST OF *SHE INVESTS!*

https://nanmckayconnects.com/2021/03/investing-in-women-silvia-mah/.

Silvia Mah

Silvia Mah's passion for empowering investment in women-owned businesses spans accelerators, incubators, a venture group, a podcast show called *She Invests!*, and a new book titled *Power of Purpose: Servant Leadership in the Startup World.*

We use two terminologies in the investment world that most people may not be familiar with. One is called an accelerator. The second one is angel. The innovation ecosystem or startup ecosystem is a community of people who are working toward a goal.

In a startup ecosystem, everybody is working around this goal of startups and access to capital collaborations between startups that can be collaborations, partnerships, and how we raise economic development in the startup industry. That's an ecosystem.

Within the ecosystem, there are different players. There are various stakeholders, investors, and entrepreneurs who do hard work right off. Some advocates are running different kinds of organizations, and there are resources. The resources could be law firms and accountants, and marketers that help the entrepreneur do their job. But these advocates that connect the system usually are running accelerators, incubators, or coworking spaces. There is sometimes a meetup type of community organization.

Accelerators and incubators sometimes are used interchangeably for people incubators. Everybody has a definition based on the industry, which may be a little bit different. Sometimes not the industry, but just the ecosystem, in general, defines it differently. Incubators for me, specifically in San Diego, are physical locations that you put your startup together, have some space, get your team together, and incubate in that space. Usually, you pay rent, sometimes not. Sometimes, space is not a physical space, but a community. Startup San Diego is a community organization. It serves as a kind of incubator plus partner of all incubators in San Diego.

Typically, when you are part of an accelerator program, it depends on whether you are scaling your business or launching your business. Usually, the accelerated text equity in your company means that it could be 1 percent to 3 percent, 5 percent, 10 percent, depending on the resources they give you. A lot of people know about Y Combinator and TechStars. Those are accelerators. Sometimes they are called incubators. Five Hundred Startups is the same way. Those accelerators take equity in the business because you're going through a course.

An accelerator like Stella Labs focused on women-led businesses, has a 3-pronged approach, where we equip women to launch and scale their startups, lead access top capital opportunities for them to gain opportunities to pitch to gender-lens investors, and build a network of mentors, advisors and advocates for more startups with women leaders to gain the funding they deserve. As our network and offerings have grown, through a robust network of investors and innovators built on trust (the most valuable currency of the funding ecosystem), Stella has added Stella Angels, an angel group for women investors to invest in women founders and a venture fund, Stella Impact Capital, to invest in women-let startups at the intersection of deep tech and impact. This is the typical network affect of most accelerators that bring a significant value-add to startups at the earliest of stages.

How can you start and get equity in something specific to product-market fit in an ecosystem without just launching it? How do you do those first very nascent steps? That is what Stella Labs does, and it's a service fee. And we give out scholarships all the time because we get funding from federal, state, and city governments. There are many ways of looking at accelerators and incubators.

* * *

ACTION STEP 26.

FINANCING AND CAPITAL

Analyze your current financing situation to determine the source of your needed capital for the business.

- ☐ I have enough savings to cover my business expenses for a year.
- ☐ I have another person in the household who can cover my personal expenses.
- ☐ I will need to seek venture capital.
- ☐ I will run this business as a side hustle until I can cover my expenses.
- ☐ I am going to take out a loan for expenses for a year.
- ☐ Other plans: ______________________________

BUDGETING

Budgeting is an easy but essential process that business owners use to forecast current and future revenue and expenses. The goal is to make sure that enough money is available to keep the business up and running, to grow the business, to compete, and to ensure a solid emergency fund. When you start out, if you are doing the business as a side hustle, you can budget your business expenses only. However, if you plan to use the business to fund your personal expenses, you at least must know what your personal expenses are running. Your revenue projections must cover not only the business expenses but also your personal expenses. In this situation, you must be especially careful that your revenue projections are based on reality.

INSIGHTS INTO FINANCIAL PLANNING

INTERVIEW WITH **TARA JONES-WILLIAMSON**,

FINANCE COACH, YOUR PRETTY PENNIES

https://nanmckayconnects.com/2021/06/how-to-make-smart-financial-and-lifestyle-choices-tara-jones-williamson/

Tara Jones-Williamson

Tara Jones Williamson educates and empowers women to move from making poor financial and lifestyle choices to intentionally manifesting their best lives and achieving financial freedom. She is a CEO, content creator, and success coach behind Your Pretty Pennies.

I created like this little mini suite of financial resources, based on the different stages women are at right now. The financial planner is a tool everybody needs because you should be budgeting your money every month. You should be tracking your financial goals and expenses. If you are not managing your money, you can guarantee that your money is managing you. I am very adamant about that.

That's why I created the ultimate financial planner with the last twelve months, so you have twelve budgets in there. Twelve expense tracking sheets has a place for you to track one short-term and one long-term goal. Every three months, you have a goal, a goal checklist, and a goal check-in to make sure you are hitting those goals.

We also have a Financial Reset Online Academy. That is my online course for individuals who are ready to hit the reset button. This is basically the step-by-step process that I went through all those years ago when I pressed the reset button on my finances. You are going to learn about creating a budget, managing that budget, creating more income streams, creating financial goals, and learning which goals you should prioritize. We are going to talk about savings, debt repayment, and similar topics. That's the financial reset.

Then we have the Financial Freedom Fast Track. It is a group coaching program/course that is a hybrid between the financial reset and working one-on-one with me. The course is for five weeks. Each week, we go through one lesson. You will listen to the lesson and do the worksheets. And then we have a Q&A session.

In week two, we do the same thing. Week three, we do the same thing with the goal of building you a two-year plan that allows you to pay off all of your debt in two years or less. That is the end of the process for the person who says, "You know what? I already have a budget. I'm serious about paying off debt. I want to get totally focused about paying off student loan debt, paying off the credit card, paying off the auto loan, whatever it looks like. I want to get hyper-focused on paying off debt."

On my website, you can find that I do one-on-one coaching where I help women and couples create a monthly budget, create their savings strategy, create their five-pronged financial plan.

* * *

ACTION STEP 27.

BUDGETING

Analyze your budget situation with the preparatory work you have completed to date.

- ☐ I have a budget that projects my business revenue for a year.
- ☐ I have a budget that projects my business expenses for a year.
- ☐ I have a budget that projects my personal expenses for a year.
- ☐ I have not made any budgets yet.

ACCOUNTING

You may be having a great time thinking about creating and delivering a product or service and neglect one of the most important areas to watch: cash flows and profits . . . the numbers. Shopify has a great article on cash flow and profits. Its formula for the number is profit = demand × revenue (less expenses). You can calculate your cash flow here: https://www.shopify.com/capital/calculator?itcat=blog&itterm=58612357

According to the Shopify blog, small businesses spend an average of $40,000 in their first year.[14] Do the math on what you think the demand will be. And remember that these are just business expenses, not paying yourself a salary. There is a great blog on the Entrepreneur's

---

14. https://www.verizon.com/business/small-business-essentials/resources/cost-of-starting-a-small-business/#:~:text=Shopify%20research%20determined%2C%20%E2%80%9Csmall%20business,on%20the%20number%20of%20employees. Direct is : https://www.shopify.com/blog/cash-flow-management

Guide to Small Business Finance at https://www.shopify.com/blog/small-business-finance.

The first step, if you are going to make the jump into entrepreneurship, is to find out, to the penny, how much you are spending and what you are spending money on. This isn't a budget. It's the real numbers. Then go back and realistically figure out if you can cut back. I hear people say, "I could live on a lot less." But when you get the pencil out and start crossing things off the list and say, "Would you really cut out that gym membership?" the answer may be different. Another way to do it is to combine making these cuts with a side hustle. Now you are getting closer to reality. But you still have a safety net—your job.

Then start on the second bucket of expenses, the costs of running the business. These costs will depend on the type of business you are considering. A service business is probably the least expensive to start. In other words, you sell your skill, labor, or expertise—instead of products or goods. An online business is probably the least expensive, but you will need programs or applications, which are almost all based on a monthly subscription amount; your website costs, which are probably going to be much higher than you anticipate; costs for any help you need, even if the people you hire are from Fiverr or Upwork; and the marketing costs.

INSIGHTS ON SPENDING

INTERVIEW WITH **RIAH GONZALEZ**,

FOUNDER AND CEO OF LINQ CONSULTING

https://trailblazersimpact.com

Riah Gonzalez

Riah Gonzalez does clear path consulting for forging and maintaining strong new relationships, re-engagement consulting for driving lasting client relationships, and virtual assistant matchmaking.

I tell people, if you have a choice, and you're planning on going into business, be more mindful about planning capital. I had a job but also had two clients, and I was under-charging significantly. I wasn't thinking they were a side job; I was doing a favor for friends. I wasn't charging like you would as a consultant. I wasn't charging as you would to make a living. I was charging as somebody doing a favor as a friend. I can't suddenly say, "Well, I got fired. So now my fees are five times the amount that you know that they were."

If you're thinking about going into business, be mindful that in the beginning years, you are not going to be able to pay yourself or the amount that you're going to be able to pay yourself is going to be very small. If you're doing it right, you are investing quite a bit of money into your business. I did not pay myself for 18 months, and that was excruciating.

And there were many financial decisions I could have done differently. I have a podcast called the Client Experience Revolution, *and I have an episode called "Sexy, Sexy Money," where I interviewed an accountant. We talked about the fact that just because it's deductible does not mean that you should buy it. You have to really think, "Do I need this thing? Is this crucial to me moving to the next step?"*

Be a good steward of the money that your business is making, because everything that you spend is $1 away from giving it to yourself. The financial is real. It is a real thing that people should not be afraid of, but be aware of because, in the beginning, it is quite a challenge. Having any savings is very helpful. Don't go out, guns blazing. And just because it is deductible doesn't mean it is a good decision.

* * *

You also need to be realistic about the revenue side. How long will it take to get the revenue to cover those reduced expenses you now have? And if you have savings, how long will the savings last to cover these reduced expenses? The rule of thumb is that your business cash reserves should equal at least six months of expenses. One to two years is more realistic because it takes a while to get a business up and running, acquire customers, establish credibility, and determine whether you have a product or service someone wants to buy.

On the other hand, if you have the financial means (another source of income) to work at a business instead of the business being the work and your primary source of income, you may be able to indulge in some of the luxuries.

Now that I have scared you to death, let's circle back. These suggestions are merely cautions and considerations. Do not let the cautions overwhelm or discourage you. You have come a long way when you are at this point in the book. You are much further ahead than most people starting a business. Entrepreneurship will bring you the promised joy.

The difference between you and a person off the street who decides to start a business is that you are approaching it strategically. You are gathering the facts. You are making a fact-based decision. By writing all this down as you create your business, you are 99 percent further along than anyone who ever thinks (but takes no concrete steps) to create a business and "go for it."

Imagine me sitting beside you with a glass of wine or juice. We are celebrating how far you have come! We are celebrating your release from whatever is holding you back. We know you can create the business you want. We know that you can have the freedom and independence you crave. We now have a plan. Keep going!

BOOKKEEPING

Even if you are small, you must track your revenue and expenses. Your choices are probably to learn a program like QuickBooks or hire a bookkeeper as a consultant. I preferred the latter because I had so many other things to learn, I didn't want to concentrate on that one.

Get your bookkeeping set up from the beginning. If you have an aptitude for bookkeeping, I commend you. However, you must ask yourself, "Am I spending too much time on bookkeeping? Is bookkeeping the best use of my time?" With a small, new company, you are the person who either must do the work or pay for it. You need to pick and choose. At first, I thought I would learn QuickBooks and bookkeeping, but I soon realized that if I spent my time learning and doing this task, I wouldn't get the product produced.

I hired a bookkeeper who has her own business to do the bookkeeping, my monthly financial reports, and the W-9 and 1099 work. I give her the monthly Excel spreadsheet of revenue and expenses. You are going to need a record of everything.

Try to charge your business-related expenses to one credit card. As a receipt comes in electronically, print out only the page(s) you need and put them in a file. At the end of the month, I review my checks issued, Payoneer if you are paying someone out of the country and not through Fiverr or Upwork, credit card statements, bank transfers, and PayPal. If there is a business expense, I find the receipt that goes with it and check the expense off the credit card. Both get scanned as backup, and every expense is accounted for.

The spreadsheet has six columns: Date, Purpose, Company, Type, Amount, and Credit Card Number. The Purpose column would state what the expense is, such as book, hosting, subscription, editing, or consulting. The Type column would be production, research, marketing, admin, or education. The Credit Card Number is the last four digits of the card the expense was charged to. I send the spreadsheet with the scanned-in receipts and credit card listing, with check marks, to the bookkeeper each month. She enters the documentation I send her into QuickBooks and prints out the financial statements for me.

ACTION STEP 28.

ACCOUNTING AND BOOKKEEPING

Explain how you will handle your bookkeeping.

My plan for bookkeeping is:

- ☐ Perform my own bookkeeping using this program: ____________
- ☐ Contact other business sources for bookkeeping leads
- ☐ Use this company: ____________________________

Explain how you will handle your accounting.

My plan for accounting is:

- ☐ Perform my own accounting using this program: ____________
- ☐ Contact other business sources for accounting leads
- ☐ Use this company: ______________________________

SALES TAX

Collecting sales tax is a major research area. Online sales flew under the radar for a long time, but most states are now aware of the online businesses and are starting to put regulations in place to require the collection of sales tax. Look at Amazon, as an example. They did not originally collect sales tax but now are required to collect it. These requirements differ from state to state. When you are doing online sales, you are in the potential sales tax zone.

I strongly suggest you research it. There is a Sales Tax Nexus Guide to review, located at https://www.taxconnex.com/sales-tax-nexus-guide. Another reference is "Online Sales Tax Compliance: e-Commerce Guide for 2021" at https://www.wix.com/blog/ecommerce/2020/12/online-sales-tax-compliance.

Look at sites like SamCart, Shopify, and Etsy, which handle sales tax issues if you use their services to sell digital and other products online.

INSURANCE

Business insurance needs vary, depending on the type of business. Insurance possibilities include general liability, property and liability, workers compensation, umbrella, and errors and omissions. One type that owners do not always think about is key person insurance.

INSIGHTS ON KEY PERSON INSURANCE

INTERVIEW WITH **JANISE GRAHAM**,

FOUNDER AND CEO OF WEALTH TEAMS ALLIANCE

https://nanmckayconnects.com/2021/04/how-to-know-yourself-and-your-history-to-move-forward-in-life-janise-graham/

Janise Graham

With more than twenty years of experience in the financial services industry, **Janise Graham,** bestselling author of "Leaving In Style: Business Succession on Your Terms," is also well versed in a variety of insurance solutions. She leverages her experience as a retirement specialist to the employees at such companies as HP, Verizon, and Avery Dennison to help entrepreneurs better understand the nuances of long-term business succession planning to protect the future of their families, businesses, and employees.

One of the biggest concerns is the lack of planning in the event of the loss of the leader. My first experience and exposure in my industry was to retirement planning. That is where my focus was until one day, I got a call from my mom telling me that her dear friend, a very successful businessman, had crashed his plane. This gentleman was an excellent pilot and would fly himself and others frequently. The events of this day changed the trajectory of my career. On a Tuesday afternoon in February 2001, this gentleman flew his young son back to the home he shared with his mom in Northern California. There was a landing strip on the property, so it was a convenient and quick turnaround trip. He then took off, heading back to Southern California, and did not make it.

After learning the tragic news, I started asking my mom questions such as, "What will happen to the business?" She did not know. So, I started asking some of my mentors in the industry. I would tell them the story of what happened. They asked about some of the things he should have had in place as a business owner but did not.

A lot of business owners are not aware that they can protect themselves from financial losses. Another challenge is that some business owners think they are invincible. They are going to be here and working forever; they are going to be healthy forever. No one wants to think of the unthinkable. Besides accidents, there are at least ten ways that I can think of that could affect a business owner's ability to work. Unfortunately, they may have no idea until it is too late.

Many business owners will consider Key Person Insurance if they know about it. Just think about it; the key person is not always the business owner. A key person can be the CEO or CFO or someone whose loss would negatively affect the company's bottom line. Suppose one of your employees is the company's "rainmaker," such as a business developer. In that case, you may consider getting a Key Person Insurance policy on that individual. You might be saying, "If that person died, my business is going to fall apart, at least until I can find someone to replace her." That is what Key Person Insurance covers. The insurance protects the business in the event of the loss of someone critical to the company's success.

* * *

ACTION STEP 29.

INSURANCE

- ☐ I have addressed my insurance needs with a qualified insurance professional.
- ☐ I have a plan to cover my lost income should I become too sick or injured to work.
- ☐ I do not have any of my insurance needs covered.
- ☐ Other: ______________________________

CHAPTER 8 TAKEAWAYS

ESTABLISH FINANCIAL SYSTEMS FOR BUSINESS STABILITY

- Startup capital—ensure you have a financial cushion before leaving your current job, or make the business a side hustle to avoid running short of capital or income.
- Have multiple streams of revenue if possible as you grow your business.
- How to build a business projected to make profits if it's not a nonprofit.
- Understanding venture capital and what it looks like for businesswomen.
- Understanding accelerators and incubators and the roles they play in financing entrepreneurs.
- How to have a strategic financial plan consisting of expenses and revenue projections.
- How to realistically approach spending in a newly established business.
- How to approach sales tax plus protect your business from financial losses through the Key Person Insurance.

CHAPTER 9

DESIGN AN EFFECTIVE STAFFING AND TRAINING PLAN

We all know you cannot do everything yourself and start and grow a business. You must divide the work. You either will hire employees, full- or part-time, or hire contractors. We have more opportunities on staffing with freelancers and contractors than we have ever had before. I recommend starting with freelancers. Many sites have all kinds of options for assistance, and you can usually find a good match. If they are not a good match, you do not have to sit down face-to-face and fire them. However, you do have to supervise them. This chapter will provide information on employees and freelancers because many of the supervisory functions are the same.

EMPLOYEES

Hiring employees or not is a double-edged sword. If you do not hire employees and try to do everything yourself, you have an opportunity cost to consider. If you do not hire people to help you, you must learn new programs and acquire new skills, and all of that takes time. Conversely, if you have employees, you may have a huge learning curve on government regulations and requirements.

Whether employees are needed depends largely on the type of business. If you have a physical storefront operation, you need employees. We are not suggesting that you always do everything yourself. If you have an online business, you can view employees differently and utilize the services of the organizations that attract and supply freelancers. These freelancers often live around the world, so you are dealing with time zones. As these services grow, the variety of services available increases.

Most of these freelancers do business with companies in the United States and make themselves available when you need them. You will probably find that you can adjust to their work time, too. The reply may not be instantaneous, but you must question whether you need immediate attention. Other than the potential of using a platform like Zoom, you communicate with this type of employee primarily through their platform, such as Fiverr and Upwork and sometimes by email. The platforms like Fiverr and Upwork prefer that you use their platform exclusively for communication. You hire and pay for them directly on the platform.

We have a variety of opinions from the entrepreneurs we interviewed. Much of it depends on size of the company, familiarity with operating remotely, and the type of business you have.

INSIGHTS ON HIRING REMOTE WORKERS

INTERVIEW WITH **CLARE PRICE**,

FOUNDER AND CEO OF OCTAIN GROWTH

https://nanmckayconnects.com/2021/01/clare-price-podcast/

Clare Price

COVID accelerated a trend that has been happening for the last ten years. People have been going into telecommuting. They have been going into remote work. There has been a big move to using contractors for many different things. My team is all remote workers and contractors that I bring into different projects depending on what the client needs.

We have incredible flexibility. I do not have the overhead of employees to have to pay salaries to or to make sure that there is enough work for them. When the work is there, I have people for it. I can also match the capabilities of my clients to the team members. They are always getting the person who is the right fit for them. That's me.

Now, in general, companies across the globe are saving money, hand over fist, with going to remote. They are saving money on office expenses. They are saving money on small things like office cleaning that they had to pay for where they are in office. They are saving money on travel—big savings! Of course, that has put a dent in our hospitality industry. For every positive, there is going to be a downside.

But they are also saving on the ability to have top talent. They can recruit their top talent across the world. If they have a programmer who is perfect for them, and that programmer happens to be in India, they can hire that person. One of the strongest benefits is the ability to have flexibility, the ability to save an operational cost, and the ability for employees to live and work wherever they choose.

* * *

Consider obtaining the help you need in doing your tasks but try to avoid hiring employees in the beginning if you can. If you pay an employee more than $600 a year, you are locked into a myriad of requirements. Unless you are working on a platform like Fiverr and Upwork, ask everyone you pay for services for a W-9 form, even if it has a business name. I did not realize the W-9 was a requirement for people with a business. At the end of the year, I had to go back and ask someone who had been paid more than $600 for a W-9, and she refused! All you can do is note it but ask for the W-9 upfront and get it before you pay. The safer route is to use Fiverr, Upwork, or a similar service. When you go through a service like Upwork or Fiverr, you can ask them about the W-9 status, but to date, I have been told the company handles the W-9s because we pay Fiverr and Upwork directly. They then provide the W-9 to the freelancer on their site. Easier and safer.

On these services, be clear about what kind of services you need. Put a request on the site, be very clear and specific about your request, and anyone interested will reply. If you find someone who can provide the services, that person is often willing to work for a monthly amount as well as a project amount. You will find you can control your costs better by paying monthly if you have ongoing tasks. Even if there is a time zone difference, you can adapt by working with them at the beginning and the end of the day. I have worked with people in Africa, Jamaica, France, and the United States. One of the concerns is whether their English is acceptable. Most of the time it is, but I recommend doing a Zoom meeting before you hire them, to determine their English capability.

Another option is to hire an apprentice through Acadium.com. I hired the first person I worked with on an apprenticeship, and she is still working for me two years later. If you find someone who is a fit for your needs, it can be a great relationship. The problem is that most of the people you hire on an apprenticeship basis require considerable supervision. You will need to lay out their tasks, explain exactly what you want as an outcome, touch base with them no less than weekly, ask for small results you can review, and praise them for their small wins. The reason you want to hire an apprentice is that the cost is minimal. The supervisory time it takes to get them ramped up is not minimal because they want to learn and become proficient in a new skill. It is very similar to hiring and ramping up a new employee in the corporate or business world.

However, even in a small business, creating a motivational environment for your employees is important. The most impressive business environment I have encountered was created by Sonu Ratra, cofounder and president of the IT consulting and talent solutions organization Akraya. She also founded Women Back to Work, which partners with many leading companies to implement return-to-work programs with roles designated specifically for professionals who have taken a career break. Her company was ranked as one of the Best Places to Work.

INSIGHTS INTO WHAT EMPLOYEES VALUE

INTERVIEW WITH **SONU RATRA**,

COFOUNDER AND PRESIDENT OF AKRAYA AND FOUNDER OF WOMEN BACK TO WORK

https://nanmckayconnects.com/season-two-ptb/

Sonu Ratra

Sonu Ratra has an industry-leading program that helps companies that value diversity and inclusion tap into the often-overlooked talent pool of career-ready returners with technical backgrounds. Her company was listed by Glassdoor as one of the Best Places to Work.

The Best Places to Work ranking did not come from me, but from the employees of Akraya. It goes back to having the right culture, the openness in the company. Every month, we share the financials of the company. We share what is good and what is not going good for the company so that people believe that this is their company. They know exactly what is happening, and they really helped move the company forward.

One innovative benefit that I should speak about is the home cleaning service that we provide for our employees. It is ranked by Forbes among the top ten benefits provided to employees. Eighty percent of our employees are women. Many years ago, we realized that our employees were complaining, especially women, that they had to go back on Friday and Saturday and clean their homes. They felt they did not get enough chance to spend time with their families. We thought it would be a great benefit if we provided them a cleaning service. It was very simple.

We have a cleaning service go to their homes to clean. That's one of the reasons why we are one of the best places to work.

You need to listen to your employees and see what it is that they need. It comes down to having an open environment. People come into the workplace to address the challenges without feeling stressed, so they enjoy the workplace. I can't tell you how many times people in the office will say, "You could take away anything, but don't take away this benefit." We have the gym membership, medical, the 401(k), and the other benefits. But this is a benefit that truly, truly matters.

* * *

Over time, or if you have the type of business that requires it, you may need to hire employees. Therefore, in this book, I have also included more information directly related to having employees on board.

INSIGHT ON HIRING EMPLOYEES

INTERVIEW WITH **SUSAN MCPHERSON**,

FOUNDER AND CEO OF MCPHERSON STRATEGIES

https://nanmckayconnects.com/2021/07/how-to-build-meaningful-connections-susan-mcpherson/

Susan McPherson

One of the greatest bits of advice I was given goes all the way back to the beginning of 2014, and I often tell it to entrepreneurs who are just starting. This is a generalization, but sometimes women—and certainly I was one of them—have the propensity to want to hoard.

This means in good times, I was going to be hunkering down, doing my work, not spending, because things were going to dry up. And I needed to have that extra, like a squirrel. I needed to have all those acorns just for the rainy day. A woman who had done sustainability consulting for many years pulled me aside and said, "Susan, this is the time you want to invest in bringing more people on, whether they're 1099 or employees, so that you can be out and about doing the business cultivation, speaking, meeting with people." I listened to her.

What I found was I could surround myself with people who love to do the things I detest, or love to do the things that I suck at. That has been I really think one of the secrets of our success. We have so much wisdom into what our talents are, but we also have wisdom into what we are not good at and what we don't want to do. When we are entrepreneurs, we have the choice. If I could try to offer some advice, it is to get out of your own way, as scary as it may be to spend money to hire people. If you do it successfully, it will free you up to follow your North Star to be successful.

* * *

VIRTUAL ASSISTANTS

Small Biz Trends has an excellent description of virtual assistants and lists forty-seven tasks a virtual assistant can do for you.[15] A virtual assistant is an independent worker who assists with administrative, business development, social media, other marketing, or other tasks. By taking on recurring tasks and administrative work, they free up time for small-business owners, entrepreneurs, and managers.

---

15. https://smallbiztrends.com/2019/09/what-is-a-virtual-assistant.html

The virtual assistant works remotely, often from a home office. Virtual assistants may be U.S.-based but may also be located in another country. Virtual assistants have become incredibly popular with small businesses over the past decade because they are a flexible workforce. A virtual assistant can be part-time or full-time, depending on your requirements. Need twenty hours a week? No problem. Need thirty hours? What about forty? Virtual assistants are available. Virtual assistants may be paid an hourly rate, or they can get paid a fixed fee per week or month.

Often you can get a better deal and deeper benefit by hiring a full-time virtual assistant, for several reasons:

- Prices can be surprisingly affordable, especially for offshore workers.
- It is easier to integrate a full-time assistant into regular workflows.
- A full-time virtual assistant will be better positioned to learn any special software apps you require, develop cordial relationships with coworkers and customers, and grow with you as the business grows.

Some virtual assistants work as independent freelancers. Others are part of a company or agency where you hire the company to provide a flexible workforce. When you work with a virtual assistant company, you are dealing with a manager who will discuss your needs and find the best fit.

INSIGHTS ON HIRING VIRTUAL ASSISTANTS

INTERVIEW WITH **CLARE PRICE**,

FOUNDER AND CEO OF OCTAIN GROWTH

https://nanmckayconnects.com/2021/01/clare-price-podcast/

A virtual assistant is somebody who basically handles, from the beginning, your office chores, bookkeeping, booking appointments, anything like that. They can be remote. I have used people who are in different areas—from New York to California.

You look for somebody who is motivated, has a good office skill set, is proactive, and looking for ways to support you.

The other thing is that a lot of virtual assistants today specialize in certain things. You can hire a virtual assistant to do outside sales calls, social media, or many different tasks. The tasks include not just office chores, but all kinds of activities that you would want to do in your business.

The value of having a virtual assistant, particularly for a smaller organization, is the overhead. They work by the hour, and you pay for what you get. They are available to increase or decrease their hours as you need.

In my case, I have a virtual team that does all my accounting. They're out of the Philippines. They happen to be a client of mine, and I have a client of theirs, and they are fabulous. They are organized. In my experience, the best virtual assistant is proactive and will look at your business and start making suggestions as to ways that you could do things differently or better. That is gold.

* * *

INSIGHT ON WORKING WITH VIRTUAL ASSISTANTS

INTERVIEW WITH **RIAH GONZALEZ**,

FOUNDER AND CEO OF LINQ CONSULTING SOLUTIONS

https://nanmckayconnects.com/2022/01/how-to-find-the-just-right-virtual-assistant-riah-gonzalez/

Riah Gonzalez

I pivoted my business, not the consulting side, because I do client reengagement consulting, which has always been a part of my business. But instead of being the virtual assistant, I now matchmake and help people find their virtual assistant in the Philippines.

We use a website called onlinejobs.ph, sort of like indie.com. I do a very detailed consultation process with the client of what it is that they're looking for. We create a job description that really draws in and attracts that person specifically. We take it from there. We list the job description; we receive the applications; we do the initial interviews; we do all the screening; we narrow the applicants down; we get sample work from them. Then we deliver a list of three candidates to our clients.

Typically, our clients are looking for a freelancer maybe fifteen to twenty hours a week. But they want to work with them long-term.

They don't want to work with them on a project base. Fiverr is fantastic. But Fiverr is really structured to be a project-based site.

These are people looking to have somebody because they can't afford a virtual assistant or don't want to pay for a virtual assistant here in the United States. They'd prefer to pay less but still have somebody very skilled. One of the beautiful things about what we do is that we're providing for a better quality of life for somebody in a developing nation.

We do the whole process with the needs in mind of the client, you know, and matching them specifically with somebody who can meet those needs. We have another list of people and process for clients who want people living in the United States.

* * *

In the beginning, if small businesses need employees, they simply need a reliable employee they can train and trust to show up for work on time.

HIRING

You need to hire the right people for the right job. If you take the job description requirements—the knowledge, skills, and abilities needed to do the job—and the job attributes into consideration, you are more likely to find the best person to fill the job. Why is this important? If you fill the job with the wrong person, just because the person you chose is ready, willing, and appears to be able, you may end up with a poor job fit and high turnover. After you have invested time and money in the hiring and training process, you will want a perfect fit to fulfill your workforce needs.

The hiring process consists of three aspects: an application, which will result in knowing whether you have workforce capability (as described above), a testing process to determine whether the person has the workforce capabilities needed, and an interview process to supplement the information gathered from the application.

Current studies reveal that the organizations with the most effective hiring policies were more likely to use the following four practices:

- Job interviews in which candidates are asked to describe specific examples of their skills
- Automated resume screening and search
- Assessments that predict whether candidates are motivated by the factors associated with a particular job or the company's values and mode of operation
- Simulations that gauge specific job-related abilities and skills

If you are hiring a remote worker from a site such as Fiverr, these are tips for successful hiring:

- Look at the number of reviews and the rating
- Review the service they are offering
- Read the "About the Seller" section for qualifications and the work
- Read their reviews from buyers
- Determine the number of orders in the queue
- Contact the seller and enter your requirements
- Message them to be sure they respond and can do what you want
- Obtain an agreement from seller before placing your order

Fiverr provides the following advice on finding the right freelancer for your project:

- Review the freelancer's work samples
- Check out the feedback from other buyers
- Choose the package that best fits your needs
- Contact the freelancer with questions to determine alignment with your expectations

EMPLOYEE/CONTRACTOR TRAINING

Providing appropriate initial and ongoing training for new staff members is essential, not only in terms of preparing individuals for their new position but also in retaining them for a longer period. Employees who are trained properly are more knowledgeable, more competent, and can meet the requirements of the job sooner.

After orientation, a probationary training period is usually in place that is specific to the position and job requirements. Training during this period is generally more extensive, as you are trying to bring the employee up to speed as quickly as possible. The focus should be on knowledge, skills, and abilities required to perform the job for which they were hired.

COMMUNICATION

The essence of communication is to make your message understood by others. There are three main types of communication, and you must master them all to be effective as a manager:

- **Written:** Correspondence, reports, email, memoranda, and other written messages.
- **Oral:** Face-to-face communication, conducting meetings, giving instructions, and training. There are two aspects of oral communication—the content of the message and how the message is delivered—and they are of equal importance. The tone of your voice directly affects *how* the message is received.

- **Nonverbal:** These are messages you send through your gestures, facial expressions, and overall body language. Body language and other nonverbal cues can enhance or detract from your message. Make certain that there is congruence between your words and your body language.

When managers fail to establish consistent communication guidelines, materials, and protocols for employees, it will lead to a significant breakdown in communication. A supervisor who is unclear about the priorities of the owner may not meet an important deadline to implement a new policy. A staff person may send an email with an inappropriate signature comment that offends a coworker. When clear communication guidelines and policies are not established, serious problems may result. Management should brand and standardize outgoing communications and provide accessible hardcopy or electronic documentation that speaks to the organization's mission, values, and services, as well as its policies and guidelines.

Too often, management learns of the need for communication by having to respond to the lack of it. The owner and senior leadership team set the expectation for effective communication through their commitment to open, honest, and timely communication. Their actions, behaviors, and messages send a strong message to supervisors and staff about the tone and tenor of communications within the company. Employees will emulate the style and tone in communication that they receive from their managers. Even if there is top-down commitment by management to internal communication systems, the success of communication will depend on the communication skills of the individuals who manage and do the work. Skills include speaking, listening, writing, questioning, and providing effective feedback.

Without effective communication, managers cannot perform the basic functions of management (i.e., planning, organizing, directing, leading, and controlling). Communication serves as a foundation for performing these functions. Managers generally devote approximately six hours per day to communicating. They spend much time on email, on the telephone or Zoom, or in face-to-face communication with their superiors, subordinates, other managers, and customers. They must use written communication in the form of letters, emails, reports, or memos wherever oral communication is not feasible. Speaking or sending a written message to others, however, does not guarantee that those who receive it will understand your meaning. Few people are natural communicators, and most professionals seek out training and education to help them improve their communication skills. They recognize that their success as a manager is directly related to their ability to communicate with others.

INSIGHTS INTO EFFECTIVE COMMUNICATION

INTERVIEW WITH **KITTY CHANEY-REED**,

VICE PRESIDENT OF ENTERPRISE OPERATIONS AND SENIOR STATE EXECUTIVE FOR IBM

https://nanmckayconnects.com/2021/02/kitty-chaney-reed/.

Kitty Chaney-Reed

One of the things I have learned that sets me apart is feedback. Dialogue with other people, be willing to connect with people, and be vulnerable. I think that applies in every situation when you're trying to solve tough problems. Ego is not something you can bring to the table. You must be humble. You must be a listener; you have to be a bridge builder.

I think over the years I have perfected that skill. You can always grow in every challenge. The skill gives you an opportunity to grow more. I think one of the things that I am known for is pushing the envelope, but pushing the envelope in a constructive way that people view me as a builder. That view is important in corporate America.

I find that this is a skill that you do not see very often. You see a lot of strong people, a lot of smart people. But collaboration and the ability to build things and build relationships is a skill that is learned and honed over many years.

* * *

INTERVIEW WITH **SUSAN MCPHERSON**,

FOUNDER AND CEO OF MCPHERSON STRATEGIES AND AUTHOR OF *THE LOST ART OF CONNECTING*

https://nanmckayconnects.com/2021/07/how-to-build-meaningful-connections-susan-mcpherson/

Susan McPherson

One thing that is vitally important is overcommunicating. When in doubt, be overly transparent. If you're not going to meet a deadline, be overly communicative with people. If an employee or freelancer is doing a good job, be overly communicative if you need to give constructive feedback. We are using modes that are not as natural as when we are in person with one another. You can read an email and take it in many ways. I think it is important to overcommunicate. Pick up the phone and talk to people.

ACTION STEP 30.

STAFFING AND TRAINING

- ☐ I am going to hire full-time staff.
- ☐ I am going to hire part-time staff.
- ☐ I will keep each staff person's earnings to under $600 per year to avoid the W-9 requirement.
- ☐ I will hire a payroll company to assist me with payroll.
- ☐ I am going to use virtual assistants.
- ☐ I don't know what I'm going to do, but I know I had better get a plan together.
- ☐ ______________________________

CHAPTER 9 TAKEAWAYS

DESIGN AN EFFECTIVE STAFFING AND TRAINING PLAN

- When you're just starting out, explore how to work with freelancers/remote workers to make your work easier than hiring full-time employees.
- Foster an open environment in which employees are listened to and feel valued.
- Understand the virtual assistants' concept and why you should consider hiring one as a new business owner.
- Research factors to consider when hiring freelancers or full-time employees.
- Consider training employees for better productivity.
- Recognize the three forms of communication and how to effectively communicate in an organization.

CHAPTER 10

CREATE AN ONLINE BUSINESS

An online business is one of the fastest businesses to launch—and grow—with the lowest risk. The steps for an online business are not much different than a storefront business. One difference is that the likelihood of having staff, especially in the beginning, is less in an online business. You are more likely to use freelancers. However, the supervision and communication responsibilities are heightened because you are not discussing your needs and expectations face-to-face.

The biggest dividing line in an online business is whether you are going to sell products or services. You want a profitable business where you are solving a problem for people, and they want to purchase whatever you are selling. You want market validation, but it is better to ask people who are not in your social circle whether they think your product or service is viable.

Remember, just like a storefront business, you want to find a need and fill the need with your product or service. Perfect ideas are nonexistent. The idea you start with will morph along the way. You will modify your idea many times, usually improving it as you go along. Waiting to get it perfect will delay your start. Better to get started, work through the action plans in this book, and see your idea start to take shape.

As you progress, you may find someone who seems to have the same business idea as you have. Do not worry too much if this occurs. Your idea will not be the same as someone else's because the way you implement the idea will be your own. Recognize that the business that was first in the market has an advantage. You will have to find your advantage, whether it is a twist on the idea of the other business, your marketing, your customer service, or whatever else might be a relevant difference.

In the beginning, you want to go as niche as possible. Start out by offering a few products or services. You can always grow. Do not try to be too many things to customers. Be lean on your initial revenue estimation.

Have a good plan of attack. Review the chapter on marketing for other areas to consider that are germane to the online business.

The most common online businesses include affiliate marketing, blogs, podcasts, YouTube videos, coaching services, consulting, digital products, drop shipping, online fashion boutique, online thrift store, flipping, graphic design, handmade products, mobile app design, online store, print on-demand products, resume building, teaching online classes, author/writer, translation, transcription, website builder, virtual assistant, and more.

The skill-building focus for your online business, in addition to the typical management skills needed, is website building and maintenance, search engine optimization, data organization and storage, content creation, email marketing, social media, communication tools, freelance identification, vetting and supervision, customer acquisition, and online marketing.

INSIGHTS ON ONLINE BUSINESS

INTERVIEW WITH **CASE LANE**,

FORMER CAREER DIPLOMAT AND FOUNDER AND CEO OF HER ONLINE BUSINESS, READY ENTREPRENEUR

https://nanmckayconnects.com/2020/08/case-lane-2/

Case Lane

I didn't know what part of online business I wanted to do right away. No, not at all. I started out on a different path. I started out writing. And I started out self-publishing. Then I started to learn about all of the online business options. I really didn't know that world at all. I didn't know what a lead magnet was or a landing page or some of these other terms that have become so popular in the online business space. I knew what a website was, but I certainly didn't know how to build my own. And I didn't know I would get lots of emails from people. I didn't know there was a whole email management system behind it. Now I've learned a great deal over the years in building my own business.

Your research should include revenue in the context of competition, startup time, and reality. If you're a professional and you're worried about how much time it's going to take you to start a business, spend the fifteen minutes a day doing the research on each of the different online business areas, or maybe a half hour or a little more as you start to pick the one that you want. Focus, just start there, just start with fifteen minutes a day of research and build from there.

* * *

APPS TO RUN AN ONLINE BUSINESS

There are so many apps today, it is hard to figure out which ones are the best and will serve your purpose. Almost all apps are now monthly subscriptions. I would advise keeping them on a monthly basis because if you pay annually, you will save some money, but you cannot cancel them midyear.

INSIGHTS ON THE USE OF TOOLS WITH A VIRTUAL TEAM

INTERVIEW WITH **CLARE PRICE**,

FOUNDER AND CEO OF OCTAIN GROWTH AND AUTHOR OF *MAKING REMOTE WORK*

https://nanmckayconnects.com/2021/01/clare-price-podcast

Clare Price

If you're going to have a virtual team, the virtual team must have a way to work together. There are wonderful virtual collaboration tools out there. As I mentioned in my book, Make Remote Work, you have to start with your foundational office suite.

You have a choice, typically, of Microsoft or Google G Suite [now called Google Workspace]. They each have their plugins. For example, Google has Google Meets for video conferencing; Microsoft has Teams. You should review some of the specialty collaboration tools that are out there. For Teams, for example, I use Air Table. And I think it's a fabulous tool to organize everything. It has a lot of templates. You can do everything, from your social media calendar to your project tracking. The other one that I really like is a tool called Whimsical, which offers you the capability of doing wireframes.

For websites, Mind Mapping, I have a mind map in my book. And I also use all kinds of flow charts with clients, such as the customer journey. You can do all of that with Whimsical. So those would be two tools that I would recommend. And the reason that you want to do that is because you want to have a way for your entire team to log on to one universe and be together. Another great tool that has exploded is Slack for Communication. Collaboration is another great tool that a lot of us use.

You can get my book, Make Remote Work, on our website, octaingrowth.com. Just go there and click to download the book. What I wanted to do with the book was to provide not just general information, but to provide relevant tools that people could pick up and use. I reviewed twenty collaboration tools and picked out one to ten that I really liked so that I could provide my clients or anyone reading the book with something that had been somewhat vetted. Monday is a great collaboration tool. A competitor of Monday is Reich, also good for team collaboration. You find a lot of emphasis put on project management, because when projects get out of control, teams start to fall apart. Basecamp is an old favorite, which has been around for a long time. But the cool thing about Basecamp is they have done a lot of refreshing to the software that they created a couple of decades ago. And it's quite a good tool. It's very competitive now. You can also sign up to book some consulting time with me if you have a specific question about the remote economy or any of the business challenges that you might have.

* * *

Some of my favorite apps which are very helpful in an online business are the following.

- **Zoom.** This app is at the top of my list because it is integral to the podcast and video business as well as webinars, summits, and course design. Most businesses will typically use Zoom in one way or another, whether it is for staff or consultant training and meetings or whether you are using it for customer service.

- **Trello.** This app is where I keep everything about guests together, from their pictures prepared in Canva to their written descriptions to their quotations to their embed codes and links—everything in one place. I have this app for about 300 interviewees. You could use this app for your customer information, too. It's a great place to organize your work.

- **Canva.** This app can be used to produce all kinds of pictures, from marketing pieces to picture cards with names on them.

- **WeVideo.** I use this app to capture a small audio quotation that can be inserted in an email.

- **Otter.ai.** This app is good for obtaining transcripts from audio or video.

- **Dropbox.** I have big files to store. I can place the files here and then upload them to my Upwork consultants.

- **Slack.** I use this primarily for group communication and getting files back and forth from my other hosts to me.

- **Upwork** and **Fiverr.** I couldn't live without these apps. Most of my consultants come through these sources. I have people who work for me doing editing, writing show notes, locating pictures, doing administrative work, and all kinds of duties but live somewhere else in the world, from Africa to Jamaica to the United States.

- **Acadium.** I have found a few people who want to do an apprenticeship for three months. If I can use this period to train people and then have them continue to do work for me, it works well. One person has been with me for over two years. However, I have found that apprentices require a considerable amount of supervision and training resources, and I usually cannot pay enough to bring them on because they want a full-time job.

I have a full list of our timesaving favorite apps in these categories and more: audio editing, course hosting, data organization, email management, freelancers, graphic design, landing pages, networking, office suite, online storefronts, payment processing, free photos, podcast hosting provider, scheduling, selling online, social media, social media management, data storage, team communication, transcription, video conferencing, video creation, website builders, and workflow. Claim your bonus at https://nanmckayconnects.com/GoldPowerBonus

WEBSITE

Creating the website should be one of the first tasks for an online business. The website will brand your site's digital footprint. Review other websites to find the look and feel that you want to project. Designing, maintaining, and hosting a website is a big expense. You may have this skill, but you should weigh the time it will take to learn the website development program versus doing it yourself. WordPress seems to be the most widely used. Our site is designed with WordPress, which allows us to select a company for website development and maintenance easily since there are many sites developed with WordPress. If you learn the basics of WordPress, you can do most of the changes yourself and, even if you change your website hosting or development company, the basic WordPress doesn't change. If you can learn to do most of the typical updating of your site, the money you save will be worth it.

The size of the site (number of pages) will directly relate to the cost, as will whether you do it yourself. I have contracted with a big firm and a small firm, and I much prefer the small firm. If they get to know you as a customer, their response time and accessibility is much better. Most of the big firms do not have website design availability on weekends for technical decisions, and weekends are often when something goes wrong. Although some website companies offer design services monthly, most do not. Even if the website vendor has a monthly service, if you have a technical problem, the vendor's weekend staff does not know how to fix it if it's fairly complex, or they are not available on the weekend. With a large company, you rarely get the same support person twice, and even if you remember them, they don't remember you. The cost is about the same with a large or small company, depending on what you want from them.

You will find it helpful to have a graphic designer and a technical website developer in the same firm. You are either working with layout and picture changes or technical issues. I use Blizzard Press, and they have both services in the same firm. They also arrange for hosting, and they perform the design and maintenance. Most of the firms do not have content writers. Therefore, you need to think about what you want to say and have a basic idea in mind. If you are going to change the look or add a feature to your website, it helps to have several sites you like as a reference.

It is not necessary to have your website maintenance and hosting done by one company. You want to have an SSL certificate for security, but most hosting services provide that either in the hosting price or as a separate cost.

ACTION STEP 31.

WEBSITE

- ☐ I have reviewed at least four websites and I know what design I want.
- ☐ I am going to design my own website and I have experience.
- ☐ I am going to design my own website and I don't have experience.
- ☐ I am not going to have a website right away.
- ☐ I am going to contract with a company to design and program my website.
- ☐ Other: ________________________________

ACTION STEP 32.

REVISE GOALS

Now that you have considerably more information about yourself and your business, you may want to revise your goals. You have conducted much more research and thought than most people do when starting a business. Choose the business that will meet your goals and satisfy your needs. You will continue to learn along the way. Set a timeline for yourself and write a short business plan. Review your personal finances and budget to determine, realistically, how much revenue you will need. Estimate your business expenses as best you can. Have enough in reserve to carry you, both personally and business-wise, for about a year. You are getting close to a launch. However, all businesses need customers, so we must next think about how to acquire customers.

GOAL #	DESCRIPTION	SPECIFIC	MEASURABLE	ATTAINABLE	RELEVANT	TIME-BOUND

CHAPTER 10 TAKEAWAYS

CREATE AN ONLINE BUSINESS

- The types of online businesses to start and the process of starting.
- Tools to use when using a virtual team, plus some of the author's favorite ones.
- How to start, design, and establish a functioning website for your online business.

SECTION III

ACQUIRE CUSTOMERS WITH SIMILAR MISSIONS AND VISIONS

CHAPTER 11

DEVELOP A SENSATIONAL MARKETING PLAN WITH A CUSTOMER FOCUS

These questions are part of developing a sensational marketing plan.

- Should I develop a marketing plan? How do I decide where and how to do paid ads?
- Who is my avatar or ideal customer?
- Will my business have traction in the marketplace?
- Should I do a newsletter?
- What marketing do I need to do?
- How do I use social media?

MARKETING STRATEGY AND PLAN

A marketing strategy is the way in which you will accomplish a specific goal. Your marketing strategy could include how you will get your message to the right audience and focuses more on the future with a long-term approach. A marketing plan, even if basic, is a helpful tool to help analyze your options and plan of action. First, do the research on what is available at what cost to compare to your budget. Then develop a plan of which marketing sources you will use on what time frame. Look at your results by quarter and decide after six months whether you want to continue with your plan or whether the outcome is not what you want and, if not, what other approach you should try.

Organic marketing refers to the act of getting your customers to come to you naturally over time, rather than "artificially" via paid links or boosted posts. Organic marketing includes anything you do not pay for directly, such as blog posts, guest posting, unpaid social media posts, email blasts, search engine optimization (SEO), interviews on podcast shows, or YouTube channels. Paid tools, such as Facebook boosts and ads and LinkedIn ads, are considered inorganic marketing. The key to the definition is "over time." As a startup, over time equates to a slow build-up. Especially if you have transitioned from a career, you will want a faster build-up than organic marketing may provide. A combined approach works best.

There are a variety of ways you can market an online business, such as email marketing, social media, podcasting, and video such as YouTube. You can market your business with a Facebook ad, a LinkedIn ad, and a Google Ad. You can weigh the cost of the ad against the benefit for your business, and depending on the ad, it may not be expensive. You typically have to have 1,000 subscribers and 4000 public watch time hours on YouTube to do YouTube ads, but you can do Google Ads with no minimum.

Paid marketing targets your customers, and you can specify which market you are targeting. The paid marketing does not have to be expensive. For example, if you boost a post on Facebook, you can edit your audience by gender, age, geographic location, and interests. When you set a budget, the Facebook site will show you how many people you will reach. You can run an ad for seven days for under $100. However, you will balance customer reach and cost. The more you spend, the more people you reach.

You often drive traffic back to your website, so having a great website that shows off your brand well is critical. Your website should include a sign-up that allows you to collect email addresses in your chosen email provider. By collecting emails through your website, you are providing a method for people to opt-in to your emails. You also are required to have an unsubscribe feature. When sending your emails, you are required to have a way to unsubscribe. Website users can purchase your products by a website cart or by connecting to your PayPal or Stripe account.

You are going to set a tone or example on your website of what is acceptable to you. Does the website have a more professional look or a kooky, rather crazy look? Is your website more appealing to women or men? Decide on your look and your tone and use the look consistently, throughout everything you do. If you want a more professional, clean look, focusing on women, you will use more white space and more quality pictures of women who represent your avatar (your ideal customer).

The reason you use target marketing is to reach the group most likely to want or need your products or services. What are the demographics (gender, age, education) and geographics (region, city, state, country) of the people most likely to purchase the item or service you have to sell? Gathering more information is an advantage, but with the concerns about privacy data today, obtaining data on socioeconomic ranges (income, education) is more difficult.

Deciding your marketing target and your organic and non-organic marketing choices in line with your budget is the basis for your marketing plan. In the beginning, the lack of experience will mean trial and error. The important factor is tracking your results to see what works and what does not work.

CUSTOMER FOCUS

Marketing is not all about you. Marketing your business is all about your customers. Who are your customers? What do they like and dislike? Who is your ideal customer? Your ideal customer is referred to as your customer avatar. A customer avatar is a representation of your ideal customer—the type of person you want to purchase your products or services. Chances are you've seen this phrase tossed around countless times, especially in terms of digital marketing.

Customer focus is a strategy that puts customers as the basis for your business decision-making, instead of focusing on profits. Customer focus is a long-term strategy that develops loyalty and builds trust. You want to discover the customers' needs to deliver premiere customer service to them and address their pain points. According to Salesforce Research, 62 percent of customers expect you to adapt to their feedback and actions.[16] If you don't, your customer will find someone who will. Customer-centric businesses are more profitable.

Customer focus will help you build relationships and help your customers to be more successful. If you have customer support tickets and a support team that answers them, go back and read them. They will provide invaluable information!

I believe in management by example. Spend time working with customers. Your employees will observe how you interact with them and will model your behavior. If you are upset about a customer and are tempted to vent to your staff, remember that you are setting the example. Complaining about a customer to your staff may give you momentary satisfaction, but the employees will think you want them to behave in the same way. While venting is not always negative, the venting could be complaining for the sake of venting and complaining to effect change.

Constructive complaining, to effect change, may be positive. The intent behind the complaint is positive when positive change is created. Consider the input that the employee, if they are venting, is giving to you. Determine whether the change recommendation can be accomplished and provide feedback to the employee. Also consider whether the venting and the complaint is a one-off or a pattern that should be addressed.

Customer expectations seem to be higher than they used to be, probably because many online businesses have been established. Customers are comparing your brand to the other companies they are doing business with and giving you a rating. The customer-focused businesses have an advantage because they differentiate themselves. According to the 2017 Gartner Customer Experience Survey, customer experience, referred to as CX, is the new marketing battlefront. Eighty-one percent

---

16. Salesforce Research https://www.salesforce.com/resources/articles/customer-engagement/#:~:text=Customer%20engagement%20has%20never%20been,to%20accelerate%20their%20digital%20initiatives.

of the people surveyed say they expect to be competing completely on the basis of CX within two years.[17] More than two years have elapsed since the survey was conducted. Do you think the competition for business rests on the customers' experience? The examples for CX efforts include defining personas and demographics, social listening, customer segmentation, user experience, and voice of the customer. CX needs to be a company-wide commitment.

The voice-of-the-customer efforts include listening to customers, markets, and employees; analyzing insights, and taking action to drive business growth. Listening to the customer is more difficult to do in an online business, whereas when people subscribe and you gather their email, that email is all you have. How do you put customers at the heart of your most critical decisions if you do not know who they are?

How do you find who your avatar is? Figuring this information out is harder than you think! But one of our guests came up with an easy solution! Most people start with some kind of analytics. The analytics you have access to could be Google Analytics, YouTube Analytics, Monster Insights, and your podcast host.

I tried to figure out what the statistics told me about my avatar but only got broad-range generalities, and the data from the various sources was inconsistent. The more privacy issues are prevalent, the less data we have available to conclude who our ideal customer is from the statistics. As I studied my website, podcast, and video analytics, I had trouble pinning my avatar down. I thought, "Is this really important?" The more I read and studied, I realized that knowing your ideal customer is very important, but the analytics may not be the best answer for everyone.

Although there was a variance from one set of data to another, I finally concluded that my primary customer was a woman over fifty living in

17. Gartner Customer Experience Survey, 2017 https://www.gartner.com/en/newsroom/press-releases/2021-11-18-gartner-survey-shows-64--of-customer-service-and-supp

the United States. Her interests were evenly split over many categories: beauty products, travel, home, garden, news and politics, finance and investing, food and dining, green living and outdoor enthusiasts, media and entertainment, and shoppers. I thought, "Other than a couple of them, that is me."

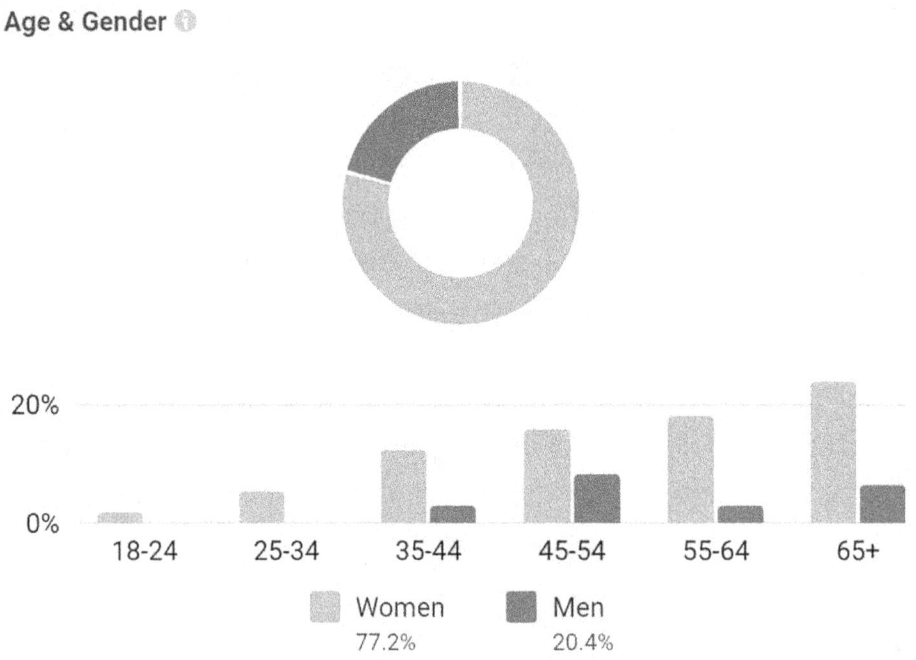

Many of the women I had interviewed fell into the category of women over fifty who had a variety of interests. Although I had interviewed women from all walks of life, I found two groups emerging for women over fifty: career women still working and retired women. In the career group, I noticed a creeping dissatisfaction and disenchantment with only having the job as their focus, which they conducted over Zoom within their four walls. During COVID-19, these career women stopped the extensive travel many of them did with their jobs. For many, the job defined who they were. I started to hear a thread of "Is this all there is?" Many women had outside interests that were directed toward empowering women and making a difference in the world.

I also looked at the retirement group, and I saw two groups there. One group was content with their retirement status and had no interest in a career or a business, but, during COVID-19, they longed for their social life, travel, seeing family, and being outdoors. The second group, confined to their living space, longed for all the same things as the first group, but they began to think about entrepreneurship and starting a business. As internet options and tools became available while they were stuck at home, they gravitated to what was possible remotely. Technology and its uses were exciting and new.

After much analysis and thought, I finally came up with my avatar: a woman over fifty who wanted to pivot from a career or retirement and start a business, preferably an online lifestyle business. What I found was the closer you get to a niche, the more you will relate to your avatar. Although I have many podcast listeners and YouTube viewers who are under fifty, we present role models for the younger group from the people we interview. And we have a few outstanding young role models on the TrailBlazers Impact Interviews show. Podcasting and video are a little different but people of all ages like stories.

When you have found your avatar, you want to identify any pain points or challenges they are having and find out where they hang out. But how do you know that from statistics? You don't. When you are running an online business, you have emails and handles, but you have little information about them. I asked the question of Joanna Bloor, and she provided that easy answer I referenced.

INSIGHT ON FINDING AND INTERVIEWING YOUR CUSTOMERS

INTERVIEW WITH **JOANNA BLOOR**,

POTENTIALIST, ADVENTURER, AND ASPIRING FAIRY GODMOTHER.

https://nanmckayconnects.com/2021/07/how-to-be-a-transformation-fairy-godmother-joanna-bloor/

Joanna Bloor

I have reached out personally to so many people who've engaged with me on LinkedIn and asked and said, "Hey, do you mind if we hop on the phone and have a real conversation?" If they are a fan of you and what you're doing, they're almost always excited to have that conversation to be part of the development of your future products and services.

Pick a social media platform, whether it's Facebook, or LinkedIn, or whatever you are using and drill down to the people who are your followers. On a one-to-one basis, talk to them directly.

I will always say at the end, "What part of this conversation was most helpful to you today?" That simple question will immediately give you what is stuck in their head. Because I come back to what I'm known for saying, which is every decision made about you and your opportunities is made in a room that you're not in. While it is about you, it is not about you or your product at all. It's about what other people in the room think.

The more you ask that question or "What landed for you?" or "What did you like?" the more useful information you will learn. I never asked the question, "What do you think?" because "What do you think?" opens the door for criticism. If you are an entrepreneur and you are trying to build your company, you hear that they are basically telling you that your baby is ugly. The hardest thing about being an entrepreneur is when somebody calls your baby ugly. You go into a confidence spiral.

* * *

What does gathering statistics on your avatar have to do with marketing? Whether you are doing email marketing, social media, or paid advertisements, understanding your avatar will help you decide what videos, blog posts, lead magnets, paid ads, and marketing campaign to use. Marketing to your avatar will even affect your email open and conversion rates.

When you send that email or make that phone call that Joanna recommends, you want to know your recipient's demographic information, challenges and pain points, goals and values, and the sources where they get their information, such as which websites, blogs, books, magazines, and movies are their favorites relevant to the products and services you offer. You want to know which conferences, webinars, and courses they attend. You want to get to know who they are and what they like and dislike. You want to know some personal information about them as well, such as their occupations and job titles. This information will assist you with your content and email marketing. The information will also help you target your online advertising. The more you know about their needs, the more likely you are to satisfy their needs.

Customers are easier to find if you solve a problem, especially if it's a small problem that could escalate into a large problem. Does the possibility exist and is the potential there? Will additional people have a similar problem in the future?

DEFINE THE CUSTOMER'S PROBLEM TO SOLVE

For my research for the topic for this book, I knew that during the pandemic, many women had to stay at home, take care of the kids, and even become online learning teachers/enforcers until schools reopened. Remote work was a necessity for many. One problem women experienced was managing the children and the inability to get out of the house to do much of anything. People started looking for entertainment that could be done remotely. Learning to do something different was interesting and gave their life a little variety. Podcasts and videos provided entertainment, and those media sources were part of my company.

People started to realize that unless they were classified as essential, they didn't have to go to the office every day. They saved money on transportation, lunches, and clothes, and they began to realize how convenient getting dressed from the waist up was when you had to go onto Zoom. When children started going back to school and most people were vaccinated, many people wanted to continue to work remotely. Not everyone, but many. The idea of starting a business began to germinate, particularly if most of the work could be done remotely. Add to that the aging and gender discrimination problems, and more women found, particularly if their children were grown, that they could pivot to a business. And another factor was the engaging thought about pivoting to a lifestyle business.

The initial problems caused by the pandemic resulted in solutions that seemed like a problem in the beginning but turned into an opportunity. People had to learn a plethora of new programs and apps, and new programs and apps seemed to spring up overnight. Zoom, Skype, Face-Time, and similar programs became a necessity, so we learned them. Social media expanded and became a necessity and a way to do business. Once we developed an expertise in the basic programs and applications, we began to think about how we could use these new tools to do something else with our lives. And then the problem morphed into

"What? What should I do? Is that struggle for promotion so important? Is there an alternative?"

Women felt an urgency in making the decision on returning to work or choosing an alternative. Would their company let them work remotely? Would working remotely for a partial week satisfy them? Would the daycare problems continue if they had children? Women in their fifties have more flexibility. Since most career women have a 401(k) and savings, would they start a business as a side hustle? Would they start thinking about the freedom entrepreneurship offers, the flexibility, and the ability to make a difference?

For these women, the problem could be defined as wanting to make a change, perhaps a pivot to a business, but what business and how to do it? For my research, I started a new playlist called Pivot to S.O.A.R., which was the launch plan for a new business or to relaunch and grow the business. I interviewed many women to gain insight into the positives and negatives. I asked them for tips for women over fifty who wanted to start a business. That data became the inspiration for my book, webinar, and course.

One way to determine your avatar, if you already have emails for potential customers, is to do a survey. Five tips for conducting a survey include:

1. Using simple, direct language. Avoid using big words, complicated words, and words that could have multiple meanings.
2. Being specific.
3. Breaking down big ideas into multiple questions.
4. Avoiding leading questions.
5. Not having more than one question within a question.

If you want to connect to your audience, ask yourself what do you want to know about them that they would be willing to provide? I had four questions:

1. Age range
2. Gender
3. Whether employed
4. Whether retired

Would a Facebook Group for your audience work for you? How could you get communication going? What would be the benefit for them? Once you know your avatar, you might have a better clue as to the next step.

If you know who opens your email newsletter on a regular basis, you could reach out to them, asking for a few minutes of their time to find out more about how they feel about your product or service.

DETERMINE YOUR TRACTION IN THE MARKETPLACE

Now that you know your avatar, you want to know whether your business has traction in the marketplace. One way is to write down five key ideas. Look carefully at the wording and phrases. Enter each of those phrases into both Google and Amazon. Do you get any hits? Are these ideas something people are searching for? The hits in both sources start to give you a picture of which words work best to describe your product or service.

I started with Amazon. I tried entrepreneur books and saw many books on this topic. I tried "lifestyle business" and saw small hits. "Lifestyle entrepreneur" was better. However, when I entered "pivot from career," I got next to nothing. I tried "women over fifty books" and got many hits, but most were for intermittent fasting. Between that and Keto, I mean a *lot* of books. What?! Is there a huge diet phase at fifty? There were quite a few on sex or historical women. I tried women over forty and saw a better variety but mostly about self-care (since we must all be starting to fall apart at forty) and staging your comeback, but that was about beauty revival.

I concluded that the general entrepreneur book field was very large. The number of books written for women over fifty was quite large, but there was no match for "women over fifty and entrepreneur." That finding could mean that there was no market for a book on women over fifty becoming entrepreneurs. Or the research could mean no one had thought of this topic yet. Or books were in the process of being written.

I decided to look at Google. If you look at Google Trends (trends.google.com), which uses search words, enter the same search words you used for Amazon and Google. You can compare your results to the Google and Amazon searches.

I did a general Google search, which resulted in more hits. From management consultants from *Forbes* to CNBC to Pinterest, people were definitely talking about women over fifty starting businesses. Did that mean that the topic was new and hot? Did the potentially new and hot topic have a shelf life? As I talk with female business leaders, I am confident more and more women will be interested in this topic.

Learning who you are going to serve and what market you are going to enter is your most important decision. When you are starting a business, you may be tempted to jump into something that sounds interesting and try your idea out. However, if you are going to leave a job and its safety net and start a business, you are wiser to take a hard look and gather your facts first. Learn before you leap. You will be more likely to succeed if you research your ideas. You now have the tools to choose the right business idea for you.

The easiest entry to a market is to develop a business in a niche market. Marketing is easier if you can focus on a smaller area and if you are known within that area and already have credibility. If you can zero in on a specific audience or can base your business with an existing audience, whether your base is an organization, an industry, or a product, people are more likely to open your email or pay attention to your social media.

INSIGHTS INTO A NICHE MARKET

INTERVIEW WITH **IRIS ANN COOPER**,

COFOUNDER OF GLORY FOODS, TRADED ON THE STOCK MARKET

https://nanmckayconnects.com/2020/06/dr-iris-ann-cooper/

Iris Ann Cooper

Some men I knew from working in a bank came to me and said, "Iris, we need some help with the marketing. We want to get into the grocery stores with a minority product, an African American product." And the rationale was that Ortega was there, but there was nothing representing Black people. And I said, "Well, how are you going to do that? My mother used to spend days cutting and cleaning greens and cooking them. You just can't put greens in a can and expect somebody to make them taste like anything if they haven't had any training.

"And I don't have the time. I'm working. I have kids. I'm married. If you're wanting to do something like that with another too-generic product, I'm not in it. You've got to find something that a person like me, who has limited time and limited skills to get dinner on the table, can get ready within thirty minutes or less, with no guesswork, pre-seasoned, ready to go."

They listened to me. They worked on the production piece, and I worked on the marketing and branding piece. I did the marketing research that proves my proposition or my assumption that women did not want to spend a whole lot of time cooking anymore at that time.

The target customer was a working woman who loved good food, loved healthy food, maybe had a family to be responsible for but didn't want to spend a whole lot of time in the kitchen. And then we tied it to the African American experience with the branding of Glory Foods—glory, meaning glorious, meaning uplifting, positive. It has a symbolic reference to religion. And it also has symbolic reference to the movie Glory, which is triumphant. And there was just no downside to that name at all. So, we went with that brand.

I did the business plan, the initial product line that we needed, and hired the ad advertising agency. My babysitter's nephew was a buyer at Kroger. And he and she hooked me up with a meeting with the buyers, Bill Williams, my partner and I, but I was the only woman and the only Black person.

A white guy and a Jewish guy hooked us up. I went in there with no handouts, no PowerPoint, no overhead projector, just talking. Just talking like this product was already there already and had the name and everything. And after I did this presentation, I asked if there were any questions. And one of the men looked around the room and said, "Well, do you all have any questions?"

Nobody said a word. Until he says, "Well, we're in. We're going to take an order, and we believe in this concept. And you'll be getting an order from us within a week or two." We had nothing but an idea. We sat in the Kroger lobby, not knowing whether to laugh or cry because we didn't even have the product at that time. Kroger waited two years until we got it. And then we finally opened at a store in Columbus in the center city in 1991.

* * *

Research is required to analyze your market. Find your competitors and review their social engagement, blogging habits, press coverage, number of testimonials or online reviews, and their search engine optimization (SEO) rankings. You also need to learn digital marketing, and one of the best sites is on Fiverr. This link will take you to their digital marketing guides: https://www.fiverr.com/resources/guides/digital-marketing. You can learn about hashtags, funnels, and many other areas of marketing.

Many new entrepreneurs lean toward paid marketing, overlooking the many opportunities for organic marketing. Do you know that 70 percent of clicks go to organic Google search results? This organic marketing equates to free marketing. Build your marketing around your avatar or ideal customer rather than around a product.

Test your market in Google Trends (http://www.trends.google.com). Add a search term or a keyword that describes your business. What would people search for to find your business idea? Note you can choose location and time frame (check over the last several years for stability). If you set your parameters as five years, you will see if the trend has been continuing or is new and perhaps not going to last for long. You want markets that are trending up or at least stable with longer-term potential. Do the highs and lows match your lifestyle schedule? Also consider the seasonality differences as they relate to revenue being higher or lower during these periods. Note that you also can compare your keyword to others, including other market areas. Generally, you are looking for stable or upward-trending markets.

You don't want a market that is too big, because the business will have too much competition and be too expensive to enter. You don't want a market that is so small that people probably are not searching for it. You are looking for something in the middle.

How are you going to sell your product or service? You are looking for long-term markets and ones that are continually relevant. You are looking for an evergreen, not a fad market, because you need sustainability. You need long-term buyers who enthusiastically want your product or service over time. Is there a club or group that would buy your product or service? Facebook Groups will provide information to research.

INSIGHT ON FINDING OUT WHAT WORKS FOR CUSTOMERS

INTERVIEW WITH **JOANNA BLOOR**,

FOUNDER AND CEO OF JOANNA BLOOR

https://nanmckayconnects.com/2021/07/how-to-be-a-transformation-fairy-godmother-joanna-bloor/

Joanna Bloor

My business for twenty-five years before this was marketing and selling things online. It is the world I have come from. If people ask me about that, my head kind of goes off, because there's so much to do here. My advice to anybody is that technology is a tool. Just because it's a tool and it's out there does not mean you have to use it.

I always sit down and say, "Okay, who are the people who are already buying me? What do they need? What are they all about? What are they responding to? How are they reacting?" If they reacted to me this way, without marketing, then maybe I will attract more people who react the same way if I market.

I fundamentally believe that not only do we as entrepreneurs offer our products and services to people but getting really clear about who you want to have choose you is equally important. Our strategies are based on wanting more customers who look and sound like this one, and what did they react to? And how do we build that?

We do it in a very experimental way. I am a startup junkie, which means that we do everything in ninety days. Sprints. I don't go all in on one decision; we do an experiment as we go. What happened? Did we like it? Was it easy for us? Was it easy for them? Did we see the results we were hoping for? Did we learn anything from this? Did this make anybody upset? Did this make anybody super happy? And did it ultimately surprise and delight people along the way?

If it doesn't come out with, "That was actually easy and fun for us. And it was easy and fun for our customers," we don't do it again. It is not about "Oh, if you do this one thing, then you're going to make it happen," because we live in a world where the choices are so infinite. If you are using everybody else's playbook, then the only thing people can compare on is price. That is a race to the bottom for everybody. It means that you are cutting value for your customer, and you're cutting value for you and then you get on that treadmill of more cutting.

* * *

ACTION STEP 33.

YOUR MARKETING PLAN

1. What is your objective? For example, if you have an online store, your objective is to sell products. If you have a podcast, your objective might be to get enough downloads per episode to attract a sponsor. The objectives for the two and, therefore, the approach to marketing and monitoring outcomes would be different.
2. Who is your ideal customer, your avatar?
3. Conduct a SWOT analysis. A SWOT analysis involves looking at your strengths, weaknesses, opportunities, and threats. This analysis is helpful when you are creating a plan. Knowing your avatar is also helpful.
4. Create a budget.
5. List five competitors and analyze their competitive status.
6. Define your strategies. Are you going to do organic (no cost) marketing or paid advertisements? Where and how often?
7. What has been your progress to date?

HOW TO USE SOCIAL MEDIA FOR YOUR BUSINESS

Social media is a fact of life in business today. For the more social types, like High Is on the DiSC profile, and the High Ss who are the relaters, this form of communication may be happiness personified. For the High Ds and the High Cs with the high task orientation, social media may not be quite as much fun. The truth is that eventually you will have to give in and accept social media. Social media usually involves Facebook, Instagram, LinkedIn, Twitter, Pinterest, and Clubhouse.

Because social media is evolving, it will constantly change. What you learn today may be obsolete tomorrow.

What do you want to accomplish with social media? If your primary focus is social connections with friends and relatives, a personal page should suffice. Remember, though, that anything you post on Facebook isn't really private. Therefore, even though you may view your page as a personal page, your page should include the professional standards you would use elsewhere in the public domain.

Facebook's primary advantage is finding connections with people who have similar likes and interests. The benefit of social media sites is that you have worldwide reach. You are no longer confined to your neighborhood to find your friends. The difference between chatting over the fence or at your child's soccer practice with another soccer mom is that social media communication is brief. The communication is in small bites with pictures, emojis, and likes. If your products or services are aligned with these likes and interests, the more likely you are to turn your "friends" into purchasers.

When you use Facebook for business purposes, you will sign up for Facebook Business Suite. Log onto the Facebook account associated with your business. You can also access the Facebook Business area from https://business.facebook.com. You can link your Facebook and Instagram accounts because Facebook owns both platforms. Business tools like posting, messaging, insight, and advertising are all in one place. Insights will show your reach and performance for both sites. You can check your analytics for both Facebook and Instagram in one place.

With the Facebook Business Suite, you can connect Facebook Messenger with your website. Your website visitors can then make a comment or ask a question, and you respond in Facebook Messenger. You also have an inbox for both Facebook and Instagram when they are connected. Comments you can respond to located in one place is a time saver!

Another connection on Facebook, for example, is Groups. Groups are available for practically any interest you can imagine. Groups can be public or private. The typical stipulation of groups is that they do not allow marketing, even from other members of the group.

The one piece of advice I hear constantly is "Don't sell on social media." The advice does not mean paid advertising is bad. What everyone means by this statement is that in your social repartee, people you are communicating with don't want to be marketed to by you. You may think, "Why else would I be on social media?" You need a fan club. You need people who like you and your products and will want to buy from you. First, they must trust you; they want to see you as a real person, not just someone selling something. Your audience wants your engagement. You are showing your personality, liking their posts, responding to their posts and comments, and generally being social and helpful.

Then, you may ask, "How do I get them to buy from me on social media?" Unless you have a unique "mouse trap" that a lot of people want to buy because your product solves a problem that other mouse traps don't solve, you have to either boost your product or place an ad that you pay for. If you want people to spend their money, you are in a different arena than giving them something for free. Video, including live video, is catching on quickly. You may want to do a Facebook Live session. Now you can connect your Zoom to Facebook Live.

My advice is don't try to learn all the social media platforms at once. Focus on one and learn that and then move to another, as you need it. I would suggest either Facebook or LinkedIn to start with. After paying consultants thousands of dollars to give me their sage advice on SEO and social media platforms, I would not advise doing this unless they take over everything on social media. That option is pricey—and your personality, which is what people want for engagement, may not come through. If you can find a great social media person to take over your accounts and post regularly for you and it sounds like you, you will probably pay about $2K per month. Many people see themselves as an expert, but their results on their own page tells the story.

Good resources for learning paths, learning labs, and courses are listed on our Favorite Apps Listing in the Gold Bonus package, which you can obtain here: www.nanmckayconnects.com/GoldPowerBonus

CLUBHOUSE

Clubhouse is a new type of social network based on voice—where people around the world come together to talk, listen, and learn from each other in real time. Clubhouse is catching on fast. Elon Musk and Bill Gates each participated, which was a major influence on the speed of acceptance. Clubhouse is a social media app for iOS and Android where users can communicate in voice chat rooms that accommodate groups of thousands of people. The audio-only app hosts live discussions, with opportunities to participate through speaking and listening.

One of the automations used in marketing and social media is the use of chatbots. Chatbots are also used to sell, to deliver content, and for customer support.

INSIGHTS ON CHATBOTS

CONTRIBUTION BY **DOROTHY VERNON-BROWN**,

GUEST AUTHOR, AND FOUNDER AND CEO OF AKB² SMALL BUSINESS MARKETING

https://nanmckayconnects.com/2021/06/how-to-excel-at-digital-marketing/

Dorothy Vernon-Brown

Dorothy Vernon-Brown is a small-business marketing strategist and coach on a mission to help local small-business owners. Dorothy is the founder of AKB² Small Business Marketing and is the co-founder of AutomateSmart.ly, which leverages the explosive power of digital automation, including emails, chatbots, SMS, and mobile wallets so that business owners can quickly grow and scale by putting their marketing on autopilot. She helps struggling business owners and entrepreneurs find effective ways to get new customers.

To fully understand what chatbots all are about, let's first define what they are. They are on websites like mine, retail stores, phone service providers—most major enterprise businesses have them. They are pretty much ubiquitous.

Chatbots can be as simple as answering frequently asked questions (FAQs) or as complex as having a "real" conversation in which you are fooled into thinking you are having a conversation with a real person. In very advanced chatbots, sometimes you can't tell the difference as they are so intelligent. Typically, chatbots in business are used to message, chat, or text.

In the same way you build an email list, you can build a subscriber list. The advantage here is that you'll be adding mobile as another way to engage your tribe. As you know, your list is one of the most valuable assets you can own in your business. Unlike having a massive following on social media, which I consider "rented property" (because the platforms are owned by the Facebooks of this world), if you get banned or suspended, you're out of luck and have no way to way to communicate with your tribe unless you transferred them over onto your list before. When you own and control your own lists, you have a business asset that can give you the best return on investment.

The bottom line is that people want to interact with chatbots. It's instant, easy, and convenient. If done right with a proper strategy behind it, chatbots can explode your sales and marketing in a short span of time with little resources behind them. You are only limited to what you can do with chatbots as your creativity. With the chatbot market projected to grow to a whopping $9.4 billion by 2024, this is a clear indication of the significant impact it will have on our businesses in the coming years. It's a win-win.

* * *

LEARN AND USE SOCIAL MEDIA

If you do not already know social media well, you will have to take the time to learn it. You can focus on one or two platforms, but almost every business needs social media in their marketing to give the business an online presence. And remember, it's very important to keep your social media updated. An inactive account is probably worse than not having one at all.

CHAPTER 11 TAKEAWAYS

DEVELOP A SENSATIONAL MARKETING PLAN WITH A CUSTOMER FOCUS

- Ask questions to develop a sensational marketing plan.
- Understand organic and inorganic marketing strategies and how both can benefit your business.
- Use targeted marketing to reach exactly who you want to sell to.
- Use the customer-focused strategy to build a more successful business.
- Define your business avatar as your primary customer target.
- Identify any pain points or challenges faced by your avatar by finding and interviewing your customers.
- Gather your customers' personal information to do targeted online advertising.
- Define customers' problems through surveys to come up with solutions.
- Determine your business's traction in the marketplace through research to understand which market you'll serve.
- Explore how to be successful in an evergreen and sustainable niche market.
- Determine what works for customers to cut you and them value.
- Utilize the five-step action marketing plan for your business.
- Effectively use social media for your business to grow successfully.
- Research Facebook and the Facebook Business Suite and Groups and how to utilize them for your business.
- Understand Clubhouse and its value—the new audio social media platform.

CHAPTER 12

EXPLODING THE GROWTH MYTH

BY GUEST AUTHOR CLARE PRICE

"Let's throw it against the wall and see if it sticks."

"Let's run it up the flagpole and see who salutes."

"We like to fly by the seat of our pants."

"Assess and pivot. It's the only way to go."

The practice is so common, so accepted, so widely used that we naturally gravitate to it. It's so ingrained in our business DNA and most of us won't know how to run our businesses without it. I know I never did! Until I learned that the pervasive business practice commonly known as trial-and-error decision-making is one of the most costly and time-consuming business crushers of all time.

It was the year 2000, the bright beginning of not just a new year, a new decade, but the new millennium, and I was working as the VP of marketing at a software startup in Mountain View, building a new analytics platform for measuring customer experience. We had an innovative product solution, a dedicated technical team, and a brash, young visionary CEO with a lot to prove to his father, one of Silicon Valley's most notable serial entrepreneurs.

Despite everything we had going for us, we started the new year in a panic. We were almost out of cash. The consumer analytics market was so new that our engineers had to innovate to create their own roadmap. And, of course, they ran into glitch after glitch on their way to success, burning through our seed funding at a rapid pace. If we didn't get a new round of funding soon, we would have to shut the doors.

We had a good track record at our stage and an easy story to tell. You can't change what you can't measure, and customers' changing expectations as the new century dawned were moving faster than ever. We had the solution!

The CEO and I met with just about every investor in town, and his reaction to those meetings shone the light of truth on the true cost of trial-and-error decision-making. Every time we met with a new investor, they had ideas about what we could do with the product and our marketing story. They weren't investing, just giving feedback.

But that didn't matter to my CEO. He'd go rushing back to me and the technical team and demand all the changes the investor had suggested, burning up more time and capital and sending the team spinning in all kinds of different directions. We never got that next round of funding. Before the sun set on the first year of the new millennium, we were out of business. And I learned a very valuable lesson.

Just about everything we believe about the value of trial-and-error decision-making is a myth. In fact, it is one of the biggest growth myths out there. But it's not the only one. Do any of the following sound familiar?

1. **Hamster wheel marketing.** Hamster wheel marketing feels exactly the way it sounds. Your marketing team is constantly running, running, running, and never seeing much of a change in new customers, revenues, and profits. Hamster wheel marketing wastes energy. The trap of hamster wheel marketing is that it gets you thinking that sheer energy will drive your business forward.

2. **Lottery marketing.** When you're playing lottery marketing, you keep putting in the coins and pulling the lever. And it works just like in the casino—often enough to keep you wedded to the lever. Lottery marketing wastes money.

3. **Trial-and-error marketing.** As I said earlier, trial-and-error marketing wastes time because you are always looking for the next big thing or buying a quick fix on impulse. When you want to throw it up against the wall and see if it sticks, you mostly end up with dirty walls. It's easy to assess and pivot your way into a financial quagmire. Sustainable growth it's not.

4. **Fire, ready, aim.** This method is to take a shot at a program or project, see how well it worked and, if it does not, then aim in a different direction. This approach wastes the tools you need to

market effectively. If one shotgun doesn't work, you try another. Then another and another . . .

5. **Make it happen.** You know you are engaged in make-it-happen marketing when you bark those words at your team and they know that regardless of the time, resource constraints, and personal sacrifice required, they must pull the rabbit out of the hat again and again and deliver the impossible. Until they don't. They quit instead. Make-it-happen marketing wastes talent, the people you count on to help you operate your business.

There are hard, painful costs to following these growth myths.

- **The customer cost.** When the organization is struggling, it creates customer churn. Customer lifetime value can be reduced by 50 percent or more as customer service declines.
- **The profitability cost.** Crisis management almost always results in project cost overruns, reducing margins.
- **The people cost.** Top talent leaves when they are overworked, frustrated, and underappreciated in a chaotic environment. According to the National Association of Colleges and Employers, hiring an employee in a company of 0 to 500 people costs an average of $7,645.[18]

Think about it for a minute. What's your process for achieving your growth vision, goals, and plans? If you're like most of my clients, I'll bet you've struggled through your share of crisis management moments, crossed-fingers guesswork, and "assess-and-pivot" top spinning.

And yes, I hear you! How do you plan for the unplannable, like the COVID-19 pandemic crisis of 2020? I believe the answer is, not with a traditional plan!

Those who weathered the COVID storm the best had a framework and structures, a system in place that allowed them to be resilient and forward-thinking, even flexible, in the face of the ever-changing dynamics of the pandemic response.

Traditional business planning has been dying for years. COVID-19 drove a stake through its heart. We have entered a paradigm shift, and the global workplace will never be the same.

---

18. National Association of Colleges and Employers https://toggl.com/blog/cost-of-hiring-an-employee#:~:text=As%20stated%20in%20a%20study,days%20to%20fill%20a%20position.

The global workplace transformation that began in March 2020 will continue. And that's a good thing. It is especially good for small- and medium-sized businesses that will need improved marketing and operational efficiencies to recover from the business disruption COVID-19 wrought.

In my book *Make Remote Work*, I highlight the changes leaders need to address in managing people for remote and hybrid work environments, improving processes and efficiencies by moving business functions and operations to the cloud, and how to design your marketing engine for the remote economy—which is here to stay.

A BETTER WAY FORWARD

The solution to sustainable growth in an ever-changing, remote-led economic environment isn't better planning, it's an operating system that supports and drives your business functions—an operating system that lays a foundation and enables your business to run smoothly. With an operating system in place, you can even manage unpredictable change.

Since early 2003 I've been developing, refining, and proving my marketing operating system, the Octain Growth System, with more than three hundred companies in twenty-two different industries. That's more than 40,000 hours of hands-on, deep-dive experience in solving real-world business problems and delivering sustainable, long-term growth for small and medium-sized businesses. My clients have spanned businesses in technology, SaaS, manufacturing, health care, transportation, financial services, and more.

In each case, we used the methodology, processes, and tools of the Octain Growth System outlined in *Make Remote Work* to deliver revenue increases of 27 to 197 percent. One client, LCS Technologies, had a three-year growth increase of 2800 percent and landed at the top of the *Inc.* 500 fastest-growth company list two years in a row.

These results come from taking control of your marketing. For most small- and medium-sized businesses, marketing is something of a black hole or a magic trick: confusing, time-consuming, and expensive.

Too often it's a drain on time, people, and resources that produces unpredictable results. I think that's why too many business owners and marketing directors result to trial-and-error tactics and crisis management that they hope, fingers crossed, will ultimately lead to growth.

What would it feel like to take on new challenges, set new goals, and know with certainty that you had the resources, the team, the time, and a GPS-quality marketing operating system-driven roadmap you could follow to achieve those dreams? What would it feel like for your team to have ultimate confidence in you as a marketing leader, with no qualms about the direction you wanted them to take?

Your time is valuable. You don't want to waste it. So, if you're ready to leave crisis management, trial-and-error decision-making behind and enthusiastically take your business in a new direction, confidently move your team forward, and see better results than you've had before, dive in and let's get started. Let's explore the Octain Growth System.

This is an excerpt from the upcoming book, *Execute2Win* by Clare Price. Reprinted with permission. To learn more, contact Clare@octaingrowth.com.

CHAPTER 13

BUILD YOUR AUDIENCE WITH A STRONG CUSTOMER BASE

To build an audience, we must have consistency in marketing as one of our top goals. Building an audience does not happen fast. You may have company pages on Facebook, LinkedIn, Instagram, and Twitter and expect that the followers and subscribers will pour in. Unfortunately, your dream will probably not be realized. The normal response to gain an audience is slow, so do not fret or immediately think something is wrong. You will have days with no new followers and subscribers. That is perfectly okay. Unless your message is terrible, your audience will build.

Start with your friends and relatives. Start building your email list by adding your contacts, friends, and relatives. You will probably be doing a newsletter. Yes, your best friend will get one. And your aunt. Your first messages may not be great because you do not yet know the rest of your audience, but you will practice. At least this audience will be tolerant. We want people to share the message, and your family and friends will more likely do your bidding and share. Plus, they are proud that you are starting a business. We want them to share the business with their friends and relatives, building a bigger and bigger audience. Ask them to listen if your business is a podcast. If you are selling something, maybe they will try your product.

Consistency and repetition are the key to building an audience in the beginning. We want to establish a pattern, an expectation, that an email about your business will be coming out on a regular basis. For example, we send our newsletter emails out every Tuesday and Friday. Your core audience will begin to expect them and look for them. Our podcast downloads are always greater on those days because the audience knows exactly what is going to happen on those days. We are building a repeating message that will grow over time. Even if the people you emailed did not open the email the first, second, or third time, they may become curious and think, "I've seen an email from them before. I wonder what it's about?" If they open the email and look at what you are offering and become a real client, they will start to expect the emails and do the right thing with them—open them and go to your offer. However, keep in mind that there is a fine line in sending just the right amount versus too many. If you send too many, your audience will unsubscribe.

One key to growing your audience is to get them to share your message. You are growing your audience exponentially if you have a good product or service because you are not telling other people about you; the original audience member is. By sending them sharable media, you are planting the seed, and they will help you grow.

INSIGHT FROM NAN MCKAY ON SHARING

> *We have a variety of ways our audience can share our podcast and YouTube channel content that you could emulate. Our website has a guest page for each person we interview. The website has social media icons that, when inserted into the website, will allow the website user to post the media directly to their own social media. If the user wants to share the guest page on their own Facebook page, for example, they can click on the Facebook icon that is embedded on the guest page, and the share will go directly to the user's Facebook account if they have one. If they want to share the link to the entire website, they can click on the Facebook icon on any of the pages of the website and go to their Facebook account to share it. The person they shared the content with can share the post again directly from their Facebook account. Our newsletter is sent in an email that allows them to simply forward the email to share. You are providing easy ways to allow the people who like your content to share it with others.*

Even though you have used easy sharing methods, the process of building your audience is not fast. Your patience will be tried—unless your product or service happens to catch on like wildfire, which we all believe will happen (but in actuality may not happen). The buildup will take more time than you are comfortable with, sometimes as much as a year. The positive is that you will figure out which method, which message, which timing works better than others. You are experimenting in the beginning, and you need to find out and focus on what works for your company.

BUILDING AN EMAIL LIST

Developing an email list is a marketing must. But how do you do that? Regardless of the business you are in, you should have a solid email list, especially including people who are interested in your product or service. Although you can buy or rent an email list, I would not recommend this. The people on those lists will not be "leads" because they have no interest in you. Building an organic email list of your own is the best methodology but building that kind of list takes time.

Your email list should be segmented to categorize the list into groups you might want to email separately. The email list should be kept clean. Delete the emails with no response. Track your email rates such as your click-through rate (CTR) for the percentage of people who clicked at least one link in your email message. To calculate your CTR, divide the total number of people who clicked by the number of delivered emails and multiply that figure by 100. Your average email open rate should be between 15 and 25 percent. Your average CTR should be about 2.5 percent. Your average click-to-open rate should be 20 to 30 percent.

The easiest way to build your email list is through your website, with a pop-up form through your email provider. The pop-up form invites people to subscribe to your website and become part of your community. Other methodologies include a free offer or lead magnet in exchange for an email address. Another method is to offer a survey or a quiz where you collect the email during the question-and-answer process. You can also offer a free summit on a topic.

One of the most popular, effective, and simplest ways to obtain targeted emails is to develop a lead magnet for an offer on your website. A lead magnet is anything offered for free in exchange for the recipient's email address. For example, lead magnets can be trial subscriptions, samples, white papers, e-newsletters, e-books, a piece of content, spreadsheets, a checklist, a case study, templates, or free consultations.

Website visitors may read a bit on your website and then leave the website. A lead magnet is designed to incentivize some portion of those people who visited your website to give you their contact information for later follow-up. If you have a product-based business, you could offer a sample of the product. If you have a service-based business, the offer could be a free consultation. Your lead magnet is something your customer would think has value. Your lead magnet should attract the right people and position those people to purchase. Who the lead magnet is for should be clear in your lead magnet marketing, addressing its key benefits. The lead magnet should have a call to action, which would be for the website visitor to enter their email to obtain the lead magnet.

A lead magnet can be used to obtain an email, but if you have a product or service to sell, your lead magnet can also turn profits for you. A lead magnet is used to get people in the door as a free give-away and you upsell to your small, inexpensive product. After they have purchased your first product, you can upsell again. You have to offer the item you are upselling right away and make your product or service very easy to purchase. For example, imagine that you have a book to sell. You also have a webinar, and you have designed a course. And, lastly, you have a coaching service. Picture a funnel. The funnel is largest at the top and then narrows toward the bottom, where only a few drops can trickle out. Your lead magnet, at the top of the funnel is a free template, for example. Then, your next offer might be a book you have written that is offered at a low cost or free with shipping and handling. If they purchase the book, the next screen takes the user to your webinar. Purchasing the webinar takes them to your course. Your course could lead to coaching or a mastermind class, or you might stop there and market coaching from your course. Each item down the funnel is more expensive.

LANDING PAGES

The next question is, where are you going to send them to take advantage of your offer? Unless you sell products and have a shopping cart or means to check out, you are going to use a landing page. A landing page is most often used to display something you are offering for free in exchange for emails. You create a landing page on your website that describes the offer and allows them to download whatever you are offering—in return for their email address or to purchase something else.

What is a landing page? Wikipedia describes a landing page[19] as:

> In online marketing, a landing page, sometimes known as a "lead capture page," "single property page," "static page," "squeeze page," or a "destination page," is a single web page that appears in response to clicking on a search engine optimized search result, marketing promotion, marketing email, or an online advertisement. The landing page will usually display directed sales copy that is a logical extension of the advertisement, search result or link. Landing pages are used for lead generation. The actions that a visitor takes on a landing page are what determines an advertiser's conversion rate. A landing page may be part of a microsite or a single page within an organization's main web site.

Landing pages are often linked to social media, email campaigns, search engine marketing campaigns, high quality articles, or "affiliate account"

19. https://en.wikipedia.org/wiki/Landing_page

in order to enhance the effectiveness of the advertisements. The general goal of a landing page is to convert site visitors into sales or leads. If the goal is to obtain a lead, the landing page will include some method for the visitor to contact the company, usually a phone number or an inquiry form. If a sale is required, the landing page will usually have a link for the visitor to click, which will then send them to a shopping cart or a checkout area. By analyzing activity generated by the linked URL, marketers can use click-through rates and conversion rate to determine the success of an advertisement.

Semrush gave four tips to developing landing pages in this article:[20]

1. **Move your call to action to the top of the page.** Place your best features and the most important information at the top.

2. **Use a high-converting headline.** Use numbers, five to nine words, multiple parts, and clear intentions.

3. **Use colors appropriately.** Read the Semrush article to see which color produces which emotion and feeling.

4. **Make yourself credible.** Use customer testimonials, reviews, and case studies to show your users that your claims are honest and forthright. Remember, what works on one landing page may not work on another, so mix it up.

20. https://www.semrush.com/blog/4-characteristics-high-converting-landing-pages-have-in-common

Once you create a landing page, you should test the landing page to see whether your page is getting the response you wanted. After looking at the results, you are going to take the highest result for the lowest cost and then use that measure as your benchmark.

MARKETING WITH A FUNNEL

The top of the funnel is for your target audience. The middle of the funnel is for your prospects or potential customers. The bottom of your funnel is for new and existing customers. You are driving traffic to the top of your funnel first. Your objective is to engage with your prospects on all levels as you provide increasing value. We use ClickFunnels to accomplish this.

The AIDA sales funnel, developed by Elias St. Elmo Lewis,[21] has become the foundation for taking potential customers through the emotional journey of making a purchase. AIDA stands for Awareness, Interest, Desire, and Action. Picture a funnel again. At the top is awareness, where the potential customer discovers you. As you move down the funnel to Interest, you are discovering their goals and problems so that you can provide preliminary solutions or quick wins. Moving on down the funnel to Desire, potential customers are convinced they have a larger problem to solve, and your premium solution is the answer. At the bottom of the funnel is Action, where the prospect decides to buy or not.

Russell Brunson is the founder and CEO of ClickFunnels, which is a great software to build funnels all while managing the backend of your products and services online. Although Brunson's funnel is based on AIDA, his funnel is slightly different because both parties are engaged in give and take. His ClickFunnels site further explains traffic and the value ladder and is well worth reading.[22]

---

21. AIDA https://www.oxfordreference.com/view/10.1093/oi/authority.20110803095432783

22. ClickFunnels https://www.clickfunnels.com/blog/sales-funnels/
https://www.itsbrandbabe.com/blog/marketing-funnel-breakdown

His approach seems to be to bring only good prospects into the funnel. Therefore, if you have an email list, and you know which people open your emails on a consistent basis and which do not, the engaged email list has better prospects for your funnel purchases, even the freebies, than the non-engaged email recipients.

You want to do automated text message follow-up. Because of the way the lead forms are set up, you will encounter form-filling. The automated text message is your primary means of communication.

To do a text, you have to gather their cell phone number which they may or may not want to provide. You can ask for it and make it optional. At the least, you can use an email sequence program like Keap to set up an automated email.

NEWSLETTER

A newsletter is an effective communication tool. A meaty newsletter, targeted to your desired audience on topics they will relate to, adds credibility to your topics.

The first step of sending a newsletter is to establish an email account. At first, I thought I would have a separate email account for this purpose because I thought I might get hundreds of emails I couldn't address. If this is your concern, you can set up a separate Gmail account for this purpose, since a Gmail account is free. I found that I didn't get as many emails as I thought I would, and I transferred to my regular business email account to send the newsletter.

You can also get an email account from a domain name provider such as GoDaddy, and then set up an account with an email provider. Many are free or low-cost and are based on the number of emails on your list. MailChimp, ConvertKit, and Constant Contact are all sources to consider.

A standard format is recommended for your newsletter, so people will recognize your newsletter by a picture or a logo at the top. Once you develop a format, you simply change the content. We want to get information into the hands of our audience on a fast but timely basis, and a newsletter serves that purpose. As you build an audience with the help from your email service provider, you can track the number of opens, bounces, and undeliverable addresses. You want to purge your email list of the undeliverable email messages as soon as possible.

Headings or subject line, images, short but impactful text bites, descriptions, and links are the key ingredients. No one wants to spend time on a long, boring, text-only email. These emails will be deleted quickly. The benefit of a newsletter is, other than the time to create it, the newsletter is free. Once you have a template, the newsletter is fast to create. This newsletter will create your early audience.

The FROM should definitely not be "No Reply." Your name or your company's name is best because you want to tie them to your company.

Think of your newsletter as a conversation with a friend. You would not open a conversation at a conference you are attending, for example, by immediately hawking your product or service. If the newsletter sounds like an advertisement selling something, it will have little traction. You are engaging your early-on customers with the plan of making them long-term customers.

Ask yourself, "What am I trying to achieve with this newsletter?" In our business, we want our audience to listen to the latest podcast, view the video on our two YouTube channels, go to our website to read the blogs, and purchase a course or book from the website. What is the outcome you want? What is your objective in creating the newsletter? Maybe you want them to share your product or services on social media. Maybe you want them to visit your website. Maybe you want them to forward your newsletter to another person. Maybe you want to let them know of an upcoming event. Maybe you want to get feedback on your idea. Within the friendly conversational tone, you want a call to action—a specific action you want them to take.

The contents of your newsletter, in this order, should include your heading or subject line, image, a welcome line with your call to action in mind, a small amount of text, and your call to action. Your heading is most important because when the person sees the email, what do they see? The subject line. We used to say, "New Episode from TrailBlazers Impact Podcast: (name of person) (heading)." We changed that to go directly to the heading as the subject line. You want something that will catch their eye so that they open it. Learn to write catchy headings for your subject line that give people a clue as to the content. Avoid the word "things." Numbers in the heading work well. Words like secrets, tips, pointers, facts, and ways work well. Trigger words like how, when, why, and what are good, but don't use more than one of these in your heading. Why would people want to read this? You want to make the reader curious about what you have to say. Another catchy title is dealing with a problem, such as "How to (do whatever)," "Here's the Best Way to," "The Best," and "Get Rid of ..." Your heading should be five words or less, if possible.

On your first few newsletters, you may want to send to a small group, including yourself if you have a second email, to be sure you don't have any broken links. Check, check, and double check for errors before you send.

How often you should send a newsletter? We send newsletters twice a week, on Tuesdays and Fridays. Our objective is to drive people to our website, a podcast site, or YouTube to listen to or watch the latest episode, read our latest blog, and purchase a course or book. We include takeaways and show notes of our episode in the newsletter that announces the new podcast and video for the week. The purpose is to pique our customers' interest in the episode we have published.

Different consultants give different answers on how often you should send an email such as a newsletter. Some consultants say five times a week is not too much. We have found that twice a week seems to be best. People can feel flooded with emails from you and not open any of them. Watch your open rate from your email provider.

You want to watch your open rate and your click-through rate. Your open rate should be about 15-20 percent, and your click-through rate should be around 2.5 percent. If you can get responses, great! If you do not get an email response, you should not be surprised, because responses are difficult to get.

ACTION STEP 34.

BUILD YOUR AUDIENCE

- What is the size of your email list?
- How do you plan to increase it?
- What is your open rate for emails?
- What is your click-through rate?
- Which social media do you use for promotion?
- How often do you post on each?
- Do you have a newsletter?
- If so, how often do you send it?
- If not, what marketing do you use?
- Do you use a funnel-building program? If so, which one?
- Have you developed a landing page?
- Have you developed a lead magnet?

CHAPTER 13 TAKEAWAYS

BUILD YOUR AUDIENCE WITH A STRONG CUSTOMER BASE

- Embark on the slow yet consistent journey to building a strong and loyal customer base.
- Learn how to start building an email list through consistency and repetition.
- Develop an email list as a marketing strategy by use of lead magnets.
- Understand how sales funnels work and how they contribute to business growth.
- Define a landing page—where they're found and their importance in the sales journey.
- Research tips on how to develop converting landing pages.
- Start and nurture a newsletter to cultivate a relationship with your audience.

SECTION IV

REALIZE YOUR DESTINY AS YOU MULTIPLY YOUR IMPACT AND INCOME

CHAPTER 14

CREATE YOUR SUPPORT SYSTEM TO PROMOTE YOUR BUSINESS

Creating a support system has been a learning and discovery area for me. Learning to lean on others may be difficult for you, too. I am extremely independent, and I have overseen everything and everyone around me for so very long. I have always said, "It's lonely at the top." Back in 1980, when I started one of my first businesses, I was one of very few women business owners. Women's organizations and women's support system groups were not available to join. My objective was to run fast and be the best. I am a High D on the DiSC profile. According to the profile, I am a highly assertive person, capable of both direct, dynamic action or charming sociability, as the situation demands. In combination, these factors describe a person with clear goals in life, with the determination and commitment to achieve them. I know I am very task-oriented and direct in my communication. After several reminders from my son, I try to start my emails with "Hi, (name)," rather than jumping directly into the email. Asking "How are you?" next in the email is not a natural inclination for me. I must continually remind myself to be social. I like efficiency, and I am in high gear most of the time. I must constantly work at patience and listening. I crave action. Perhaps many entrepreneurs fit this mold. Therefore, I felt I should write a chapter about developing a support system, which may not come naturally for other entrepreneurs.

I honestly did not know how to develop a support community. What is a support community? The Google answer is, "A support system is made up of individual people who provide support, respect, and care. These people are in your corner. Your support system does not judge you or ridicule you. These friends provide feedback that is genuine and in your best interest." I get that on a personal level. I have a group of friends I consider my support system. We get together on Zoom every other Wednesday night, but we talk about personal topics, not business. This group participation probably counts as practice to developing a support group for business.

How does a support system relate to business? My Google answer was, "They are sources of encouragement, ideas, referrals, and resources. Additionally, they give you feedback, constructive criticism, and guidance. Regardless of what stage your business is at, you're going to need support. It's best to establish your support systems as soon as you consider starting your own business."

With insights into a business support system, I hope you can develop your own system faster than I did, and the experience will probably be more rewarding. You can spend your time cultivating the relationships as you grow your business. Networks for support come in a variety of forms today: mentors, coaches, online groups, social media groups, professional organizations, and mastermind groups are some of the options women have today to develop their support systems. You also want people who will hold you accountable for completing short-term projects, such as knowing you well enough to know when you need a reminder. My biggest liability is distraction by a shiny object. I have so many avenues I want to take, so many new courses or websites or actions I want to pursue, that I can get distracted in a nanosecond. I can think of three friends who remind me of this when they hear me talk about another venture, another option, another avenue, another shiny object. I grudgingly acknowledge their feedback and go back to the project I know I must finish first. These mentors know that this direction to me is what I need.

I did not realize how WIIFM (what's in it for me) is critical in business. The WIIFM principle helps you build your sales message around what is important to each customer. Be sure to avoid the common mistakes that many sellers make when presenting their sales message, such as talking too much, using jargon, and presenting in feature language, rather than describing benefits. Each time you communicate a decision or rationale, think about the WIIFM for the other person. What will engage your audience? Explain why your solution solves their problem. What is that potential customer or client looking for when they encounter you or your product or service? You have to ignore yourself because you are not the target audience. How can your business help them achieve their goals? How can you pose your message to directly relate to the customer's needs? Not what they want. What they need.

The best way to respond to the WIIFM question of the customer is to clearly emphasize the benefits of what you are offering and how your offer is different from that of your competitors. How does your offer solve their problems and meet their needs? If you do not answer that question quickly, you will lose that potential customer. The attention span of the world today seems to be a nanosecond.

I confused benefits with features. I thought that if I explained the features, the customer would automatically understand the benefits. No. Do not describe the features of the product. Instead, describe what the result of using your product or service will be. Describe what a potential customer or client is looking for when they encounter you.

If you must change your frame of mind, as I did, a mentor or coach may be your answer. A mentor usually doesn't charge; a coach usually costs money. A mentor must not only have experience in the area in which you are interested but must also be willing to spend their time to help you. By providing guidance and information, a mentor can shorten your learning curve dramatically. The mentor also knows you well enough to suggest when you are not focusing or taking an action you should not be taking. In working with a mentor, show your interest in them and what they are doing as well, thinking of it as a two-way street. A mentorship is a reciprocal arrangement. In addition, if you are cognizant of the amount of time spent with you, be considerate of their time.

On an ongoing basis, many entrepreneurs hire an executive coach at some point. Some hire the coach at the beginning of the journey; others have executive coaches throughout their journey. As I said at the beginning of this chapter, "It's lonely at the top." The decisions you make have a ripple effect with consequences.

INSIGHTS ON EXECUTIVE COACHING

INTERVIEW WITH **THRESETTE BRIGGS**,

FOUNDER AND CEO OF PERFORMANCE 3

https://nanmckayconnects.com/2020/06/thresette-briggs/

Thresette Briggs

An executive coach can help guide you through a process to see yourself through a different lens, and to shift to the mindset, actions, and behaviors that will enhance your success. The value of having an executive coach is a critical component for this that too many business owners miss, that can ultimately be the difference between success and failure.

* * *

Coaches can help you develop, both personally and professionally. Coaches abound today, in the forms of business coaches, life coaches, and personal coaches. Be sure the people you are investing in will help you get to your desired outcome. If you are unclear about your outcome, you may waste time and money. You can fire your coach if they do not provide the services you need, but if you have established a relationship, the firing is more difficult to do.

One more support vehicle to mention is mastermind groups. These groups are designed to both help you move forward professionally, as well as keep you accountable. The group can be paid or unpaid, meet over the internet or in person, and can be long-term or short-term. The key is to hold regular meetings, with each person having a chance to contribute.

DEVELOP YOUR NETWORK OF CONTACTS

How can you use your network of contacts to find new business? The strategy needs to be mutually beneficial. Remember WIITFM?

Start with your friends and family who will support you and appreciate the idea of starting your business. When you share content on your social media, ask them to like it and share it. Sharing is a positive on social media! When they share, friends of their friends may like your media as well. You can leave your business card with the professionals who assist you, like your lawyer, your accountant, your banker, your beauty salon. Let them know that you will refer their business to others. Inform your contacts in Microsoft Office or whatever platform you use about your business and your offerings. If you can, engage your contacts with your content and build a relationship. Building your network is all about building relationships.

INSIGHT ON USING YOUR CONTACTS

INTERVIEW WITH **SUSAN MCPHERSON**,

FOUNDER AND CEO OF MCPHERSON STRATEGIES

https://nanmckayconnects.com/2021/07/how-to-build-meaningful-connections-susan-mcpherson/

Susan McPherson

The first thing I did when I started my business was to send an email to everyone I'd ever met. I said, "For the time being I'm opening up a consultancy. Here's what I'm going to be focusing on. If you know of anyone that has interest in the following, please let me know." I had created something on Twitter, called CSR chat, which stood for corporate social responsibility chat. And it was essentially a way to connect people who work in corporate responsibility. The second thing I did was continue to do those CSR chats to continue that community building. Twitter is a very different place today. But there was a time when those Twitter chats were really powerful to get your name out there to build community. The people I've served on boards with, the people who have been clients over the years and various other roles; those were the people whom I turned to for help.

Ask for help. Many of us are afraid to ask for help, but people generally want to be helping. Tap into communities, such as LinkedIn groups, but there are also many community organizations. There are so many women's organizations that you can join, whether it's the League of Badass Women or the Riveter or the We Suite, Female Founders Collective. These are all ways to tap into others, so you don't have to be going it alone.

CHAPTER 14 TAKEAWAYS

CREATE YOUR SUPPORT SYSTEM TO PROMOTE YOUR BUSINESS

- Approach building a support system through coaching, mentorship, and mastermind groups.
- Develop your network of contacts starting where you are.

CHAPTER 15

CARE FOR YOUR MENTAL AND PHYSICAL HEALTH TO GUIDE YOU TO PRODUCTIVITY

To an entrepreneur, self-care may be one of the most difficult tasks. Many entrepreneurs are task-oriented, and we often place ourselves last in line. Self-care does not equate with selfish. Self-care simply means maintaining your physical and mental health for optimal productivity. I, too, have trouble with this concept. If you enjoy what you do and you are task-oriented, work is not drudgery. Work is more of a fascination, especially if you are intrigued by creating something new. When time crunches occur or when too many unplanned factors are competing for my time, I can get stressed. When I get stressed, I talk more assertively, and others may hear it as aggressive. A strength overused becomes a weakness. I feel I am only lining up the tasks and the people to do the tasks, but the directive tone can create problems in communication. Especially if the person you are directing is a family member. So, what to do?

1. Recognize when the stress is creeping up and take action.

2. Employ relaxation techniques immediately. Close your door, if you have one, and give yourself five minutes to relax. I like to close my eyes. Once you practice relaxation techniques, you can relieve the stress in less than five minutes. You are going to use those five minutes anyway, either by directive speech, yelling, or some other emotional outlet. If you use those five minutes productively, the end result will be far more effective. You will have to practice achieving that level. You need to slow your breathing rate and your heart rate, which will lower your blood pressure and bring your mind and body back into balance. Most people start with a relaxation recording that talks you through slowing down. Smartphone relaxation apps are a good resource. A very helpful article can be found here: https://www.helpguide.org/articles/stress/relaxation-techniques-for-stress-relief.htm

3. Deep breathing, progressive muscle relaxation, and visualization are great techniques. For visualization, think of a place where you have been very relaxed. The place could be anywhere because you are in your head. You want to fixate on a place to go back to that place every time.

4. For longer-term, not in-the-moment relief, try scheduling a facial or massage. I prefer facials, but a hot stone massage does wonders too!

Everyone gets overwhelmed. Being overwhelmed, and therefore stressed, is natural and normal in the entrepreneurial world. You have a thousand things going on at once, or at least it seems like it. However, you do not need to take overwhelmed to the stressed-out level. How do you take care of yourself to avoid it?

Work with Your Energy Cycle. Your body has natural rhythms called energy cycles. You have heard people say, "I'm a morning person" or "I'm a night owl." Throughout your day (or night), your energy level cycles up and down. When your energy cycle is up, you are at your peak of accomplishment. When it's down, your body wants to rest and restore itself. Maximizing your peak cycles will gain you better productivity. Instead, if you try to force your cycle into another pattern like you might have in your college days studying for a test, you may be productive short-term, but that high energy will not last. Paying attention to your energy cycle will allow you to consistently perform at your peak over long periods of time.

Discover your energy cycle by planning it out. Learn your energy cycle patterns. As you are plotting your energy cycle, be aware of your eating and drinking behaviors. If you write this down over a few days, you will discover your pattern. Knowing your pattern is a huge benefit because you can plan your work and your meetings accordingly. If you have a very important meeting with a client, for example, you want that meeting held at your peak time, not when you are trying to stifle a yawn. If you have a complicated project to work on, you want to be at your peak performance.

When you are in a down cycle, you should avoid powering through it if you can. Those down cycles can create problems for you, because, as that task-oriented entrepreneurial personality, you want to get more done. Those times are the danger zones for eating, drinking, or taking medications to stimulate yourself and try to trick your body into working longer. Instead, try taking a walk, using your relaxation techniques, or even taking a short nap. Your energy can be restored, and then you will be ready for your high-energy cycle time.

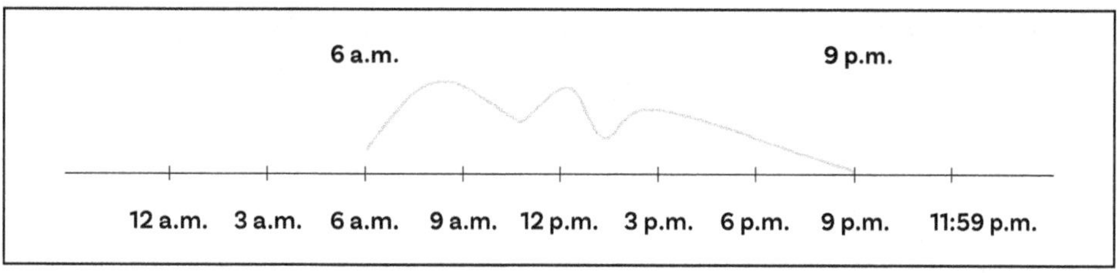

The energy cycle starts with the time of day you arise and extends to the time of day you go to bed. When I wake up, I am wide awake and ready to go. I immediately get a cup of coffee, and now I am raring to go. About 10 a.m., I experience a dip, and I start looking for food or another cup of coffee. Those activities give me a little boost that lasts until about 3 p.m. Another dip at 3 p.m., when I again look for food or something with caffeine in it. I may get a little boost, but it's downhill from the end of the little boost until bedtime. By 7 p.m., I give up. I play a game or watch a Netflix episode.

ACTION STEP 35.

YOUR ENERGY CYCLE

Draw your own energy cycle. Draw a line from your get-out-of-bed time to your go-to-bed-time using the chart below. This will help you schedule your most urgent and important tasks at your most productive time. Then ask yourself the questions below.

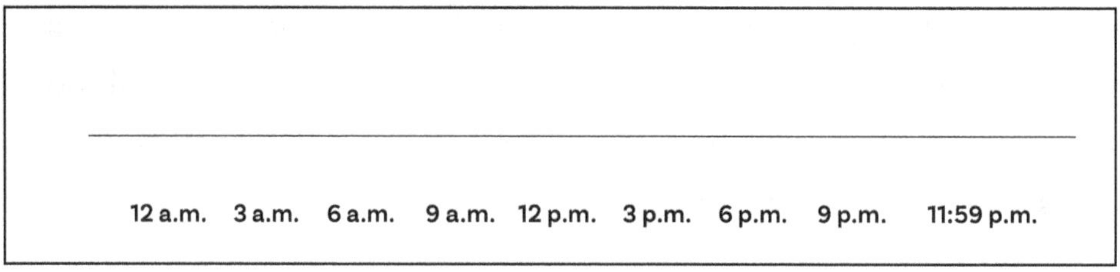

12 a.m.	3 a.m.	6 a.m.	9 a.m.	12 p.m.	3 p.m.	6 p.m.	9 p.m.	11:59 p.m.

Looking at the energy cycle you drew, when should you schedule your most urgent and important tasks?

____

____

What can you do to be productive during your low energy times?

____

____

Establish a Routine. A routine should be a productive one that benefits you the most and will allow for the greatest productivity. For example, since 3 p.m. is my low-energy lag time, I am better off doing the less critical, more routine tasks. You could even put it on your calendar. Establishing a routine need not be a strict schedule that nothing interrupts. We all know that is not possible. However, if you use your low-energy cycle for responding to social media, doing your research, and other low-energy tasks, you can better avoid performance load. Performance load occurs when you are juggling too many tasks at once. Your performance can decrease because the load is simply too much. Handling too many tasks is not sustainable over a long period of time, and mistakes will happen. Balls will get dropped. If you do not set a limit or stop when you know too many balls are in the air, your available energy will be gone. When you know you are approaching rust-out, you also know burnout is not far behind.

I find a routine helps, even in setting a time to retire to bed at night. Since I'm up between 5:30 and 6:00 in the morning, at night I am dog tired. I can push it until I am beyond tired or do the smart thing, which is to go to bed at 8:00 p.m. and read a fun, take-me-away book for 30–45 minutes. If I follow this routine, I am much more likely to bound out of bed at 6:00 a.m.!

Time Management. "Time management" is the process of organizing and planning how to divide your time between specific activities. Good time management enables you to work smarter—not harder—so that you get more done in less time, even when time is tight and pressures are high. Tasks can be divided into three categories: Important and Urgent, Important, and Routine. These categories are referred to as A, B, and C priorities.

A priorities will lead to significant consequences if not done today. A priorities are often large in scope, and we sometimes put them off because we think we don't have time to do them. An A priority might be to prepare a budget or a report for your boss or a major client. The answer to dealing with an A priority is to use the Swiss cheese theory—take little bites out of it to move it along until the A project does not look overwhelming. For example, you could gather up last year's budget and compare it to last year's expenses. You could write a section of the report.

B priorities may have a mildly negative consequence if the activity is not completed today. A B priority could entail calling a customer about a complaint.

C priorities are routine, and no penalty will be assessed if the task is not completed today. These priorities are usually easy to do, and fast. However, C priorities are usually more numerous than the A and B priorities. You can accomplish many C priorities in a day. You will feel like you really accomplished a lot because they were numerous. Concentrating on C priorities does not help you in the long run, because, by doing those priorities, you neglect the A and B priorities which are more important.

You may use one more category, the D priority, which includes those items that can be delegated to someone else.

If you coordinate your A and B priorities with your energy cycle, you will find you are more productive.

Time management is similar to the 80/20 theory. Focusing 20 percent of your efforts on the A priorities to create 80 percent results and matching that to your energy cycle will lead you to optimal performance and a better quality of life.

Part of time management is learning to say no when you know you should. Honestly, you can say no in a nice way, such as, "I would love to do it, but I don't have extra bandwidth right now." If you don't set your boundaries, other people will set them for you. Everyone will end up frustrated because you either do not get to the task they want you to do, or you do not do it well. If you know it is "too much," say no. You are not saying no to the person. You are saying no to the task.

TIPS AND TRICKS

Running a business takes time and effort and can become all-consuming. Consider being aware of when your circumstances seem overwhelming and try a few tips and tricks to keep your life in balance and maintain your health.

Physical self-care includes getting adequate sleep, eating healthily, going to the doctor on a regularly scheduled basis, taking your pills, and, yes, exercise. Walking around the block, walking around your house, staying out of the kitchen, doing jumping jacks—anything you can do to break up your day. If you can, get yourself in an exercise routine, even yoga; we all know exercise is good for us.

Keeping your stress under control definitely benefits your health! If a situation seems to cause you stress, consider changing the way you respond to the situation. You cannot be at your most productive if you are stressed out because task concentration is difficult if you are stressed. I light a Serenity + Calm candle during the day. Take deep breaths. Do relaxation exercises. Stop looking at your email every minute.

If you eat at your desk or grab something on the run, the weight comes on easily—and off hard! Behavior modification says to eat at the table and dedicate the time to concentrate on what you are eating and chewing. And drinking. Emotional snacking is common. Maintaining a food journal, such as entering your food into a weight-loss app, is useful to keep a check on yourself. Drink water. Sometimes I think I am hungry, but then a glass of water suffices. Sometimes I am simply looking for an excuse for a break. Focus on fruits and vegetables, not fast food. Power down at night with a good book. The best advice I find is to laugh—even if it at yourself. A couple of good sites with helpful self-care tips are https://www.verywellmind.com and https://www.entrepreneur.com/article/326643.

Create a workspace you look forward to entering. As an entrepreneur, you spend considerable time in your workspace, so make it yours! Pictures, books, tools you need—make it yours! Try to keep the clutter at a minimum. If at all possible, have a door on the workspace that you can close.

ACTION STEP 36.

GRADE YOUR SELF-CARE

Circle A, B, C, D next to the box, with A being the highest grade. Enter the grade for whatever you feel is best for you.

- ☐ A B C D Awareness of self-care
- ☐ A B C D Practice relaxation
- ☐ A B C D Exercise
- ☐ A B C D Sleep
- ☐ A B C D Eat fruits and vegetables
- ☐ A B C D Hydration
- ☐ A B C D Treat yourself
- ☐ A B C D Create workspace you love
- ☐ A B C D Be creative
- ☐ A B C D Facial or massage
- ☐ A B C D Fragrant body lotion after bath or shower
- ☐ A B C D Spend time outside or in nature
- ☐ A B C D Have a mini self-care session with candles, soothing music, relaxation techniques
- ☐ A B C D Take deep breaths
- ☐ A B C D Meditate
- ☐ A B C D Limit screen time

- ☐ A B C D Limit checking emails and texts
- ☐ A B C D Spend time reading for fun
- ☐ A B C D Cuddle with a pet or a person
- ☐ A B C D Listen to music
- ☐ A B C D Declutter your workspace
- ☐ A B C D Bake or cook
- ☐ A B C D Get organized
- ☐ A B C D Laugh

CHAPTER 15 TAKEAWAYS

CARE FOR YOUR MENTAL AND PHYSICAL HEALTH TO GUIDE YOU TO PRODUCTIVITY

- Prioritize self-care as an entrepreneur without thinking it's selfish.
- Reduce stress as a business owner.
- Take care of yourself to avoid overwhelm.

CONCLUSION

You have arrived! You have worked your way through the S.O.A.R. Launch and Growth Plan and are ready to enjoy the fruits of your labor! The final step is to celebrate and enjoy your new lifestyle. The journey has begun.

Being an entrepreneur has a sense of adventure about it. You know that the business can rise or fall based on your actions. Business may be feast or famine. Times are good, or times are not so good. When you are passionate about the business, you become creative about finding solutions. Each day is a new day, and if you love what you do, you look forward to that new day.

Make your life easy! Register for our course, Gold in the Golden Years MasterClass, and you can work through this blueprint step by step. Nan hosts a monthly group meeting with this class so you can focus on your Action Plan Workbook with her.

WHAT TRAILBLAZERS IMPACT ENTREPRENEURS LOVE ABOUT BEING ENTREPRENEURS

> "I love seeing a new pathway to service in community, gathering support for the mission, enlisting colleagues in collaborative effort where everyone's talents make a difference, and celebrating our outcomes!"
>
> —Lyn Burton, President and Executive Director of
> Affordable Housing Connections in the
> greater Minneapolis-St. Paul, MN, area.
> The firm focuses on affordable housing compliance
> with federal and state requirements.
> https://nanmckayconnects.com/2020/07/lyn-burton/

* * *

"Being a successful entrepreneur is not a destination; it's a journey of risk-taking and learning experiences comprised of facing and overcoming challenges. Being an entrepreneur is often nerve-racking and scary. Still, a consistent effort, talent, and a strong desire to contribute meaningfully to the world will ultimately lead to success and satisfaction."

—Cathy Light, Founder and CEO of Lideranca Group, the parent of four strategic brands: Assessment Leaders, Leadership Balance®, Be Well Perform Well, and Diversity, Equity & Inclusion. https://nanmckayconnects.com/2020/12/increase-performance-with-dei-podcast-cathy-light/

* * *

"I love being an entrepreneur because I like the direct impact I make with my clients and how they appreciate my help and the results they receive."

—Rosemarie Harris, Secured Systems Consulting. https://nanmckayconnects.com/2021/03/how-to-start-a-niche-business-without-fear-rosemarie-harris/

* * *

"I love being an entrepreneur because I can control my time, my money, my day. I love the flexibility and being able to work from home. Being an entrepreneur requires more working hours each week, but it is work that I love!

—Barbara Daniel, Publisher, and Editor of the *Cleveland Women's Journal*, a digital and print magazine. https://nanmckayconnects.com/2020/06/barbara-daniel/

* * *

"I love my work. I love the connections that I make with people. I love my family. I love my significant other. I have an opportunity to go to so many amazing places in the world. I've taken my mom on those trips; I've taken my sister on those trips. Both of my sisters have had children whom I just adore like my own. This has been an excellent year to remind me that I'm not doing enough connecting with them when I'm flying 300,000 miles a year. It's been a great year for reconnecting with what I love most. And the second thing I love most is anytime I can be outside and near the water, so I live on a lake. I have a boat on a lake and vacation in Maui whenever I possibly can. Anytime I can be on the beach or next to a river, fishing in a river or on a boat waterskiing, anytime I can be by the water, I feel like I'm at my best. That is the freedom and flexibility a business gives me."

—Cat Crosslin, Founder and CEO of InStar Performance. https://nanmckayconnects.com/2021/05/how-to-be-the-maker-of-champions-catherine-crosslin/

* * *

You now have control over your own destiny. You can create and innovate without feeling guilty. You will be constantly learning and growing.

Entrepreneurs are a unique blend of risk-takers, mad scientists, hope addicts, inventors, and magicians. They can make incredible love partners if you know how to crack the code that unlocks their love and devotion. If you don't, they can seem like the most selfish, narcissistic, unavailable workaholics you've ever met. You can be on an adventurous ride of your life filled with excitement being with an entrepreneur lover—or on a ride of terror that you want to exit ASAP.

Entrepreneur magazine has a great article titled "In a Relationship with an Entrepreneur? Here Are 10 Things You Should Never Say."[23] My comment is, "LOL. Good advice."

ACTION STEP 37.

ENTREPRENEUR LOVES

Why do you think you will love being an entrepreneur? List all the ways! And enjoy! And invite me over for a glass of wine to celebrate!

CONCLUSION TAKEAWAYS

CELEBRATE AND ENJOY YOUR NEW LIFESTYLE

- Focus on your growth mission.
- Enjoy the entrepreneurial journey.

---

23. https://www.entrepreneur.com/article/298744

PRAISE FOR NAN MCKAY

* * *

Nan may not remember the first time we met; I was a student in one of her classes. I was so excited to take the class, as Nan was known as a primary source of good, solid information in the housing industry, as it relates to Section 8 and public housing. Even in that one-day class, I could see her energy and her passion for helping others. Time passed, and I went to work for her company, only to find a structural shift the very first day, resulting in Nan herself being my immediate boss. I was able to see and experience firsthand her ability to lift people up, helping them to see the best in themselves and how to bring that best out. As a manager in her company, I found myself often applying her approaches and strategies to identifying and resolving issues. I even picked up some of her language. For example, to make sure you understand what someone is really meaning to say, I've used Nan's approach of saying: "So, let me be sure I understand," and then repeating the message back to them in my own words. Not only does this result in either agreement or a correction of your understanding, but it also underscores that you are genuinely wanting to understand the message.

Nan has moved out of the day-to-day management of her company into this new venture, and our relationship transitioned to a deep and longstanding friendship. Nan's core passion remains the same: helping others to succeed. Nan will help anyone in any way she can and thrives when mentoring others. Her enthusiasm and positivity are contagious and are evident in her podcasts, in her writing, and in her regular conversations. While it is true that what I learned from her regarding housing regulations has led to my successful career, what I've learned from her as a person has impacted my life in even more meaningful ways. I've learned how to better overcome challenges, both personally and professionally. I've learned techniques to grow my skill sets—yes, both personally and professionally. And I've learned how to look at the very best people have to offer rather than focus on the negative. She's a problem solver who believes in taking action and who helps others see what the course of action is and how to act on them.

Nan has always been a teacher. That legacy continues. It is so exciting to see her light up talking about this venture and to hear her confident optimism as she shares her life knowledge and her entrepreneurial experience with others. Nan has a fire within, and I love seeing her setting others alight with her passion.

—Teri Robertson, Senior Consultant
Nan McKay and Associates

* * *

I am the in-country facilitator for the Institute for Economic Empowerment of Women for more than six years and the founder and CEO of IWEI (Ineza Women Empowerment Initiative), registered in Canada, which helps integration for newcomers to Canada, and I served as the board member in the Private Sector Federation of Rwanda.

When meeting Nan McKay three years ago during our leadership development at AT&T's campus in Dallas, I was impressed by how humble and patient she was when staying with us at the campus, taking pictures while seated in a tiny room during the day and giving interviews to each woman present from Rwanda and Afghanistan. For many of us, her podcast was the first one we had ever been on. It was fun to see how Nan was patient when trying to listen despite English being our third language.

Everyone who interacted with her was always blown away by her passion and enthusiasm to listen to our life and business stories.

It is truly a privilege and honor to recommend her, and I can confidently say that she is a person of entrepreneurial spirit. Ever since we first met, I have always been impressed by her TrailBlazers Impact Interviews to help women utilize what they have learned throughout their careers to extend their knowledge any other way. I assure that her commitment and experience to her professional career, as well as her high moral values, are certain to all of us who follow her podcasting interviews and read her books.

I look forward to continuing to learn from her.

—Chantal Munanayire, In-Country Facilitator
Institute for Economic Empowerment of Women

* * *

When I first met Nan McKay back in 1986, I was a newcomer to the affordable housing field, and she was a giant in the industry. A person with high energy, a big personality, and a heart to match, Nan took me under her wing and was ever so patient explaining the programs and rules that went along with them. Thousands of housing professionals can credit Nan for their vast program knowledge. The first company she founded in 1980—Nan McKay and Associates—started with a handful of employees and now counts over 2,000 employees in ten cities. Over the years Nan has founded five other companies that have exemplified her commitment to empowering women, either through her company or through her training. Her new book, *Gold in the Golden Years*, is the natural next step in helping women live their best lives. Our friendship has spanned over three decades, and I am still learning from her.

—Denise B. Muha, Executive Director
National Leased Housing Association

* * *

At a time when Black female entrepreneurs are launching more businesses than ever before but continue to run into barriers that impede their success, Nan understands the problems and provides solutions by sharing her own challenges and success stories. Not only is Nan a changemaker who has achieved great accomplishments as a business owner, but she directly supports, equips, and mentors women over fifty years old in an effort to help them grow their businesses and be a viable force in the business community. Nan's book is one of inspiration and motivation and gives women a better understanding of the best ways to secure their business's financial future.

—Virginia W. Harris, Immediate Past President
National Coalition of 100 Black Women, Inc.

* * *

Anything by Nan McKay is something you don't want to miss! A celebrated serial entrepreneur, she is a singular voice on the ways women succeed, at any stage in life, and she's shared her wisdom again with *Gold in the Golden Years*, an inspirational guide to making the most of our accumulated wisdom after fifty. A must-read!

—Jennifer Brown, Founder and CEO
Jennifer Brown Consulting;
Author, *Inclusion: Diversity, the New Workplace & the Will to Change* and *How to Be an Inclusive Leader: Your Role in Creating Cultures of Belonging Where Everyone Can Thrive*

* * *

It is a privilege to meet Nan McKay since she is a trailblazer, influencer, and altruist. She founded her eponymous company, Nan McKay and Associates, four decades ago. Her company's mission is strengthening neighborhoods with collaborative partnerships.

I was delighted to be interviewed by Nan for her TrailBlazers Impact series "Pivot and Soar" podcast. We shared stories about pivoting away from our careers to another venture by creating a business. In true Nan style, she wanted to interview me about my upcoming book, *Clicks, Tricks, & Golden Handcuffs*, and highlight my journey as a former technology sales and marketing executive to a pivot as a career coach for technology executives.

I cannot wait to receive my copy of *Gold in the Golden Years* regarding Nan's journey. I feel fortunate to have crossed paths with Nan, who is a tireless crusader for female empowerment!

—Monique Montanino, Founder
Resumé Tech Guru and
Certified Executive Coach

* * *

Nan is a consummate professional who is driven to make a difference. We have collaborated on her TrailBlazers Impact podcast for a couple of years, and I have always found Nan to be brilliant, encouraging, knowledgeable, and inspiring. Her new book, *Gold in the Golden Years,* is extremely relevant in times like these. We women, of a certain age, need to find ways to support ourselves whatever the future may bring. Nan provides us with the blueprint to do just that. As always, Nan comes from a place of wisdom, experience, practicality, and confidence. I couldn't be more grateful that she has decided to share these important insights with the world.

—Donna Miller, Cofounder and CEO
Purse Power, Inc.

* * *

The True Trailblazer, Nan McKay, just does it. She is a force, a tremendous communicator, a brilliant visionary, and a focused talent full of more energy in her mind than anyone I know. I have to say, she just gets it, does it, then starts again. Her latest bold and inspiring successful business is because of her generous heart and soul to tell stories of courageous woman who have made an impact in thousands of lives. I am in awe! We met through the Women's Presidents Organization and she called out of the blue to interview me about a book I wrote, *My Living Legacy: A Personal Journey to Guide Loved Ones* (Amazon), and discovered yet another journey I am on called iPlaid.org, which raises awareness and much-needed funds for pancreatic cancer researchers through my art after losing my husband to this silent killer. Thank you, Nan; you make a difference for many.

—Susan Fielder, Founder and CEO
Susan Fielder Art

* * *

Nan is a well known champion of women and has been very much so for over fifty years. After providing housing and social services to low-income women, Nan cofounded the first Women in Housing group in Minnesota. Established in 1980, her company, Nan McKay and Associates, employed and trained women for successful management positions.

Her latest venture, Nan McKay Connects, promotes women's achievements through her podcast and YouTube channel, Trail-Blazers Impact Interviews. Her fabulous new book, *Gold in the Golden Years*, focuses on helping women over fifty create a new life through entrepreneurship and assisting current women entrepreneurs in growing their businesses to a new level.

As a founder of six companies, Nan has a unique understanding of the challenges women entrepreneurs face and provides information to leap over the obstacles to success. Nan was NAWBO's 2019 California Woman of the Year, and she has two buildings named in her honor for her service to low-income families.

—Leslie Andrachuk, Cofounder and CEO
Alpha Woman

* * *

Nan McKay is a proven success in the world of entrepreneurship and business development. Her business interests and documented performance spans fifty years, with a range of businesses: retail, catalog sales, software development, and sales; professional development; and program management. She graduated the first business from her basement into a major employer of more than 2,000 persons in multiple locations nationwide. Nan has also "built and sold" business ventures. In short, Nan, "walks the walk, and talks the talk." This book and her course provide valuable insights into the world of entrepreneurship, providing tips and techniques to dodge the pitfalls and maximize the lessons learned.

—DeLois Strum, Founder and CEO
MD Strum Services

* * *

Nan has championed women for over fifty years. In 1963, she provided housing and social services to low-income women, working directly for housing authorities for over seventeen years co-founding the first "Women in Housing" group in Minnesota. Through her company, Nan McKay and Associates, she employed and trained women for successful management positions. Her Nan McKay Connects company promotes women's achievements through her podcast and YouTube channel, TrailBlazers Impact Interviews. Her book, *Gold in the Golden Years*, focuses on helping women over fifty create a new life through entrepreneurship and assisting current women entrepreneurs to grow and take their businesses to a new level. Since Nan is over fifty and has founded six companies, she understands the challenges women face and provides information to leap over the obstacles to success. Nan's goal is to help women utilize what they have learned throughout their careers to deploy that knowledge in a new way, thereby ensuring income to sustain themselves. Nan is an inspiration—she was named NAWBO's 2019 California Woman of the Year and has two buildings named in her honor for her service to low-income families.

I look forward to being invited to the book launch.

—Barbie Siefert, Chief Advancement Officer
Junior Achievement of Washington

* * *

Gold in the Golden Years is an awesome book. The catalogue of accomplished and successful women who contributed to this book is impressive. Nan McKay has compiled an encyclopedia of personal stories, quotes, recommendations, and practical actions for women who are fifty-plus to launch a business. As a career and college readiness author, I learned some great tools for moving beyond internal uncertainty and external naysayers to enrich my professional goals as a business owner. If you are in doubt of the way forward to become an entrepreneur, this book is a must-read.

—Valarie R. Austin
Author of *The Student's Comprehensive Guide for College & Other Life Lessons*;
military veteran; business owner;
career and college readiness speaker and blogger;
and host of the Employer Speaks series,
a YouTube.com career interview show

* * *

Nan is a trailblazer! She has championed women for over fifty years. As far back as 1963, she provided housing and social services to low-income women, working directly for housing authorities for seventeen years. Nan co-founded the first Women in Housing group in Minnesota. In her company, Nan McKay and Associates, established in 1980, she employed and trained women for successful management positions. The book *Gold in the Golden Years* focuses on helping women over fifty create a new life through entrepreneurship and assisting current women entrepreneurs in growing their businesses to a new level. Since she is herself over fifty and has founded six companies, she understands the challenges women face and provides information to leap over the obstacles to success. Her goal is to help women utilize what they have learned throughout their careers to deploy their knowledge in a new way, thereby ensuring income to sustain themselves as they grow older and to have some fun traveling. Thank you, Nan, for championing women in so many ways!

—Françoise E. Lyon, President and Managing Partner
Arethusa Capital

* * *

Nan McKay is a force of nature. Ever since she was a young career woman breaking through barriers in the housing authority world, she has been a make-it-happen person.

Over the course of her life, she started six businesses, which takes a lot of gumption, vision, and tenacity. I especially relate to her work she does through Trailblazers Impact Interviews. The women she showcases, who have built on what they've learned from the corporate world and then deployed that knowledge into new endeavors, truly inspire me.

How fortunate we are that she has taken these stories like these and added her own wisdom and experiences in her book, *Gold in the Golden Years.*

—Joyce Feustel, Founder
Boomers' Social Media Tutor

* * *

I've been a colleague of Nan McKay since the mid-1970s. She was a pioneer as one of the first women to head a public housing agency in Minnesota and to lead the Minnesota Chapter of the National Association of Housing and Redevelopment Officials (NAHRO). She and I cofounded Minnesota Association for Women in Housing, which became an organizing vehicle for supporting women's career development among those employed in affordable housing private industry and all levels of the public sector. Nan is an inspiring figure to all who know her. Her insightful vision for how to make the world better for all; her entrepreneurial spirit; can-do attitude; collaborative, inclusive, and empowering style; motivational yet supportive presence; and remarkable work ethic uniquely equip Nan to pass along life lessons for all of us women in our golden years.

—Lyn Burton, Executive Director
Affordable Housing Connections,
AHC Education and Leadership Center

* * *

Nan McKay encourages women to go after their dreams and leave their mark on the world as entrepreneurs no matter their age. Her lifelong commitment to helping people lift themselves to better circumstances is inspiring and aligns deeply with my company's values of empowerment and equity through education. Nan's book, *Gold in the Golden Years: How to Launch and Grow an Online Business You Love to Make Your Own Gold*, is an insightful and necessary read. Through it, she shares valuable guidance gained from her vast and varied experiences and motivates readers to take life-changing action.

—Cathy Light, Founder and CEO
Liderança Group

* * *

Nan is a trailblazer within her own right. From her time with the Dakota County Housing Authority to owning her own company, Nan has shown women everywhere that "it" can be done. Whatever "it" is for you, you can do it. You can be loyal to an organization that also returns your years of service with learning, growing, and strengthening opportunities. You can start your own company, own it, and manage it at the same time. You can uplift other women without shrinking yourself.

Earlier this year, I was interviewed by Nan McKay as a Trailblazer for her podcast. What an affirming and encouraging moment! We shared and exchanged like old friends. Our discussion was fluid and conversational. We easily transitioned from topic to topic. Because of Nan's ability to relate and connect, we were, in turn, able to relate and connect at many levels while also discovering how much we had in common either through interests or contacts.

I am super excited to support Nan in the release of her book, *Gold in the Golden Years*. She is proof positive that while the Pot of Gold may be found at the end of the rainbow (and she is far from that in a literal sense), it is each golden nugget that you uncover and discover along the way that fills that Bucket of Joy.

—Tammi Davis, President
The Compliance Consultants

* * *

Nan is very personable, with a goal of helping women. She inspires women and gives them hope. Because of her business experience, she not only understands the challenges of women, but she helps us overcome these challenges. She is also a tremendous connector. Where there is a need, she connects you to resources that can help.

—Jayne Beckendorf, Marketing Director of BF Farms,
Founder and CEO of OSAAT,
National Marketing Director with Juice Plus+

www.ingramcontent.com/pod-product-compliance
Lightning Source LLC
Chambersburg PA
CBHW082003190326
41458CB00010B/3050

* 9 7 8 1 9 5 6 6 4 9 8 6 4 *